W9-AZP-537

THE BASICS OF WRITING

Book 2

Don L. Wulffson

Globe Book Company, Inc.

New York / Cleveland / Toronto

DON WULFFSON teaches English, remedial reading, and creative writing at San Fernando High School in Los Angeles. He is a graduate of the University of California at Los Angeles, where he later conducted postgraduate research in education.

His awards of merit include the Distinguished Achievement Award from the Educational Press Association of America and the Leather Medal Award for poetry. Mr. Wulffson has been distinguished as an Outstanding Educator in America.

He has authored 14 books for young people, 10 learning programs, and more than 300 stories, poems, and plays for a variety of publications, both adult and juvenile.

Consultants:

Dr. Vivian Grano, Ed. D.
Executive Assistant to the Superintendent
The Office of Manhattan High Schools
122 Amsterdam Avenue
New York, New York

Constance Hill
English Department
North Junior High School
Colorado Springs,
Colorado

Editors: Nancy R. Hitchner and Andrew P. Morris
Photo Editor: Adelaide Garvin Ungerland
Illustrations: Gerald Smith
Text Design: Barbara Bert, North 7 Atelier, Ltd.
Cover Art: Gerald Smith
Typesetting: York Graphic Services, Inc.

Photo Acknowledgments: Page 15—Brown Brothers; 40—U.S. Information Agency; 49—Frost/Michael Murphy (Texas Tourist Development Agency)

Other Acknowledgments

"The Almost-King of the United States" and "The Valley of the Statues," reprinted by permission of *Read* magazine, © 1983, *Weekly Reader* Publications

"A Battle Won by Toy Soldiers," from *Child Life* magazine, copyright © 1982 by Benjamin Franklin Literary & Medical Society, Inc., Indianapolis, Indiana. Reprinted by permission of the publisher

"Before Starting," from *Come As You Are*, copyright © '58 by Walker Gibson, courtesy Hastings House, Publishers, Inc.

"Earhart, Amelia," from *The World Book Encyclopedia*, © 1985 World Book, Inc. By permission of World Book, Inc.

"The Last of His People," from *Bestseller* magazine, by permission of David S. Lake Publisher

"My Land Is Fair for Any Eyes to See," reprinted by permission of the Jesse Stuart Foundation, Judy B. Dailey, chair, P.O. Box 391, Ashland, KY 41114

Poems by Robert L. Stevenson, from *A Child's Garden of Verses*, by Robert Louis Stevenson. Courtesy of Charles Scribner's Sons

ISBN: O-87065-345-8

Published simultaneously in Canada by Globe/Modern Curriculum Press. Copyright © 1986 by Globe Book Company, Inc., 50 West 23rd Street, New York, NY, 10010. All rights reserved. No part of this book may be kept in an information storage or retrieval system, transmitted or reproduced in any form or by any means without the prior written permission of the publisher.

PRINTED IN THE UNITED STATES OF AMERICA   1 2 3 4 5 6 7 8 9 0

CONTENTS

1

"BRAINSTORMS"

Imagine a make-believe world inside your head. Maybe it is a dark forest or an amusement park—or perhaps even a tin-can factory!

A group of students in Dover, Delaware, was given outlines of heads. They were asked to describe make-believe worlds inside them. Here are the results.

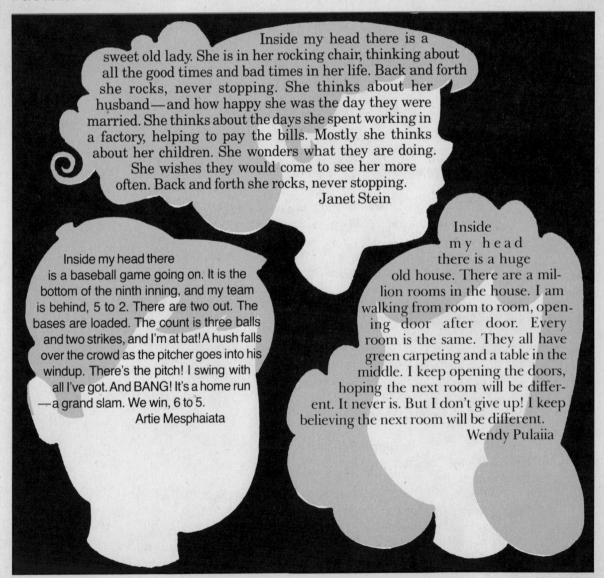

Inside my head there is a sweet old lady. She is in her rocking chair, thinking about all the good times and bad times in her life. Back and forth she rocks, never stopping. She thinks about her husband—and how happy she was the day they were married. She thinks about the days she spent working in a factory, helping to pay the bills. Mostly she thinks about her children. She wonders what they are doing. She wishes they would come to see her more often. Back and forth she rocks, never stopping.

Janet Stein

Inside my head there is a baseball game going on. It is the bottom of the ninth inning, and my team is behind, 5 to 2. There are two out. The bases are loaded. The count is three balls and two strikes, and I'm at bat! A hush falls over the crowd as the pitcher goes into his windup. There's the pitch! I swing with all I've got. And BANG! It's a home run —a grand slam. We win, 6 to 5.

Artie Mesphaiata

Inside my head there is a huge old house. There are a million rooms in the house. I am walking from room to room, opening door after door. Every room is the same. They all have green carpeting and a table in the middle. I keep opening the doors, hoping the next room will be different. It never is. But I don't give up! I keep believing the next room will be different.

Wendy Pulaiia

THINKING ABOUT WHAT YOU HAVE READ

Answer in complete sentences.

1. Which "brainstorm" shows care for another person's feelings? Use details from the writing of your choice to explain your answer.

_____

_____

_____

2. How does Artie make his "brainstorm" exciting? Give examples from his writing to help prove your answer.

_____

_____

_____

3. Which of the three writings, do you think, is the most imaginative? Give reasons for your answer.

_____

_____

_____

4. Which "brainstorm," do you feel, is the most interesting? Why does it interest you more than the others?

_____

_____

_____

5. A *topic sentence* states the main idea of a paragraph. What is the topic sentence of each "brainstorm"? Write each sentence on the lines below.

_____

_____

_____

_____

THINKING ABOUT WRITING

Word Order in Sentences

The three sentences below are made out of the same words. Still, they differ from each other in an important way.

The report is here.
Here is the report.
Is the report here?

The difference between the sentences is found in the word order. Because the words are arranged differently, each sentence conveys a slightly different meaning. Each would be used in a somewhat different situation, as you can see in the following examples.

I.

Rewrite each numbered sentence that follows, using a different word order. Words may not be added to or removed from the original sentence. (If you create a question, be sure to use a question mark.) Be ready to explain how the different word order changes the meaning of the sentence.

EXAMPLE: What they wanted was this.

This was what they wanted. OR *Was this what they wanted?*

1. Soon the bell for this class will ring.

_____

4

2. They all were frightened.

_____

3. Inside my head there is a baseball game going on.

_____

4. There are a million rooms in the house.

_____

5. They are already talking about it in Washington.

_____

II.

Write two sentences that have the same words but different word orders.

_____

_____

III.

Read the following pairs of sentences. The first sentence in each pair is all right as written. But in the second sentence, in *italics,* the word order is awkward and inappropriate. Rewrite the second sentence to improve the word order. One sentence has been rewritten for you.

1. Inside my head there is a playground. *On the swings the children are playing.*

The children are playing on the swings.

2. Inside my head there is a book. *The pages I keep turning.*

_____

3. Inside my head there is a dog. *Barking is it into my ear?*

_____

4. A cow and a moon are in my head. *Over the moon the cow jumps.*

_____

5. In my head there is a radio. *An old song it is playing.*

_____

Sentence Order in Paragraphs

The **topic sentence** of a paragraph states the main idea. It tells what the rest of the paragraph is about. Like the words in a sentence, the topic sentence of a paragraph can be moved to create different effects. For example, notice how the following paragraph can be put together in a different way.

    a. Inside my head I keep my car. My car is candy-apple red. It has a huge engine, overhead exhausts, and hydraulics.

    b. My car is candy-apple red. It has a huge engine, overhead exhausts, and hydraulics. The one problem with my car is that it is only in my head.

I.

Go back to paragraphs *a* and *b*. Underline the topic sentence in each paragraph. Then answer the following questions, in complete sentences.

1. In your opinion, which paragraph about the car is more effective? Explain why.

    _____

    _____

2. In your opinion, is the topic sentence more effective at the beginning or at the end of the example paragraph? Explain why.

    _____

    _____

3. Why, do you think, did the writer change the wording of the topic sentence when moving it to the end of the paragraph?

    _____

    _____

II.

The topic sentence appears at the beginning of the following paragraph. After reading the paragraph carefully, cross out the topic sentence. Then rewrite it at the end on the lines provided. You will probably want to make some changes in the topic sentence when you rewrite it.

    There is a crazy forest inside my head. Flowers can talk. Rocks can hop around on their own.

And trees sometimes dance with each other. _____

_____

Getting Ready to Write

On page 8 you are going to describe an imaginary world inside your head. The following activities will help you get ready to write.

I.

Listed below are *persons, places,* and *things.* In each list, circle one item that you'd be interested in writing about.

PERSONS	PLACES	THINGS
skier	kitchen	flowers
singer	hotel	treasure
child	football field	time machine
clown	tunnel	bracelet
painter	gas station	makeup
race-car driver	swamp	train
U.S. president	moon	airplane
explorer	hospital	stairs
piano player	forest	windows
carpenter	school	telephone

II.

The three items you circled are going to be the basis of the make-believe world inside your head. Think about the items. What connections can you make among them? What imaginary relationships come to mind? (For example, let's say you circled *race-car driver, moon,* and *treasure.* Perhaps you want to write about a *race-car driver* on the *moon* who is driving around looking for buried *treasure.*)

On the following lines, jot down some ideas about the items you circled.

_____

_____

_____

"Brainstorm" Writing

Now it's time to write your own "brainstorm." Inside the head on page 8, write a paragraph that describes an imaginary world inside your head. Be sure to include a topic sentence. Use your answers to "Getting Ready to Write" (above) to help you get started.

SKILL BUILDING

Nouns—Common and Proper

A **noun** is a word that names a person, place, or thing. The three lists in "Getting Ready to Write," Part I (page 7), are made up of nouns.

One way to find out if a word is a noun is to see if it makes sense with the word *the* in front of it. For example, notice how *the* fits in front of some of the words below but not in front of others.

the ask   the stapler   the your
the write   the eat   the changes

This test shows you that only *stapler* and *changes* are nouns.

I.

Each of the following sentences contains one noun. Rewrite each sentence on the line provided, placing *the* in front of the noun.

    EXAMPLE: They made dinner. *They made the dinner.*

1. Ashes were all over. _____

2. They live in apartments. _____

_____

3. He loves children. _____

4. I drew pictures for her. _____

5. She just sat there and read poems. _____

_____

Because it can be used to help you spot nouns, *the* is called a *noun marker.* The words *a, an, his, her, my, your, their,* and *our* are also noun markers.

II.

Rewrite each of the following sentences, substituting *a, an, his, her, your, their, my,* or *our* for the word *the.*

    EXAMPLE: *The* cat is up in *the* tree. *My cat is up in your tree.*

1. *The* teacher asked if *the* book was new.

_____

2. *The* coat is in *the* car.

_____

3. *The* woman suddenly ran into *the* room.

_____

4. I think *the* basketball is under *the* bed.

_____

5. *The* paper and *the* glue are in *the* tote bag.

_____

9

The nouns you've studied so far are called common nouns. A **common noun** names one or more in a general group of persons, places, or things. A **proper noun** is the name of a particular person, place, or thing. Proper nouns are always capitalized.

Common nouns: woman, moon, book
Proper nouns: Eleanor Roosevelt, Michigan, *The Scarlet Letter*

Unlike common nouns, proper nouns usually cannot be spotted by using noun markers.

III.

Read the following selection. Capitalize all the proper nouns. Also capitalize the first word of every sentence. The number of words that need to be capitalized in each line is given at the right. The first line has been done for you.

Alice in Wonderland

you have probably read the book *alice in wonderland*. but what do you know about the (4)

man who created this great fantasy? his name was charles lutwidge dodgson. the story of his (5)

life—and of his writing of *alice in wonderland*—is as interesting as the book itself.   (2)

   charles dodgson was a mathematician who lived in england during the nineteenth century. (3)

he loved to make up fantasy worlds inside his head and tell imaginative stories to children. (1)

one day he took three little girls on a picnic. one of the little girls was named alice lidell. after (5)

they ate, dodgson made up a story in which he used little alice as the main character. after (3)

hearing the story, alice begged dodgson to write it down. (2)

he did. when he had finished, dodgson showed the story to mr. and mrs. lidell, alice's (7)

parents. they, in turn, showed it to a novelist of the time, a man named henry kingsley. kingsley (4)

urged dodgson to publish the story. (1)

dodgson agreed to publish his book, but he did not want anyone to know he had written it. (1)

he made up a pen name. he called himself lewis carroll. at the same time, he changed the (5)

book's name from *alice's adventures underground* to *alice's adventures in wonderland.* (6)

IV.

How many common nouns can you find in the "Alice in Wonderland" story?
Circle at least 20.

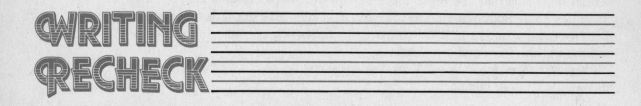

THINKING ABOUT WRITING

1. Study your "brainstorm" on page 8. Do you see ways to improve the word order in any of your sentences? If so, rewrite those sentences on a separate sheet of paper.

2. Where is the topic sentence in your paragraph? Would it be more effective in a different place in the paragraph? Try rewriting your paragraph on a separate sheet of paper, placing the topic sentence somewhere else in the paragraph.

SKILL BUILDING

3. On the following lines, list five common nouns from your "brainstorm," on page 8. Write a noun marker before each noun.

_____

_____

4. Give your "brainstorm" one final check. Be sure you've capitalized all proper nouns and the first word of each sentence in your paragraph.

BEHIND THE HISTORY CURTAIN

We asked a group of students in Jacksonville, Florida, to imagine a curtain. Behind the curtain was a famous person from history. To get facts for their writing, they did a bit of research. Then each student wrote a description of the person he or she had chosen to place behind the imaginary curtain.

Names could not be given. The idea was to write such a good description that the reader would be able to figure out who the famous person was, using nothing but the facts and the details.

Read each description that follows. See if you can figure out who is behind the writer's "history curtain."

THE HISTORY CURTAIN

This woman is probably the most famous nurse in history. She was English. During the Crimean War she saved many lives. She did this mostly by using lots of soap and water and lots of common sense. After the war she went back to England. She lived there like a hermit for the rest of her life. Can you guess who this famous woman is?

Sheila Solkoweitz

Behind the curtain is the most famous queen of Egypt. She became Egypt's queen at the age of 14. An interesting fact is that she was not Egyptian. She was part Greek, part Macedonian, and part Persian. While she was queen, Julius Caesar fell in love with her. Can you guess who this famous woman is?

Tammy Jenkins

This man was the 38th president of the United States. His name originally was Leslie King. His parents were divorced about two years after his birth. His mother remarried, and he was renamed after his stepfather. For a while he worked as a model. Then he went into politics. He became president when Richard Nixon resigned. He was our only president who was not elected either president or vice-president. Who is this former U.S. president?

Andrea Macros

THINKING ABOUT WHAT YOU HAVE READ

Answer in complete sentences.

1. What is the name of the nurse described in the paragraph by Sheila Solkoweitz?

_____

2. What is the name of the famous queen described by Tammy Jenkins?

_____

3. Who is the U.S. president described by Andrea Macros?

_____

4. What have you learned from the paragraphs? Explain your answer.

_____

_____

_____

5. In your opinion, are the paragraphs more or less interesting because the name of the person being described is not given? Explain your answer.

_____

_____

_____

THINKING ABOUT WRITING

Selecting Details

When you go to a store, you buy only things you need and want. Otherwise, you are wasting your money.

Writing is a bit like shopping carefully. You want to tell your readers only what they need and want to know. Otherwise, you're wasting words.

The following paragraph describes a piece of sandpaper without naming it. Notice that each sentence appeals to a different sense—touch, taste, smell, hearing, and sight. Notice also that three of the sentences are not needed. Can you find those sentences?

(1) Anyone who works with wood uses the thing I am describing. (2) This thing probably tastes awful, though I've never tasted it. (3) It is thin and flat. (4) It is smooth on one side and very rough and gritty on the other. (5) I don't think it has a smell. (6) It feels smooth on one side and rough on the other. (7) When it is being used, it makes a swishing, scraping noise.

Sentences 2, 5, and 6 are unnecessary. There isn't much to say about the taste (sentence 2) and smell (sentence 5) of sandpaper. Such details do not give the reader any useful information about the object. The sixth sentence simply repeats details already given.

I.

The following paragraph describes Thomas Jefferson without naming him. Cross out the *five* sentences that you think are the least helpful in figuring out who is being described. (There are no truly "right" or "wrong" choices for this activity. However, some sentences are clearly less helpful than others. Be ready to explain why you crossed out the five sentences you did.)

Can you guess the person I am describing? This red-haired, freckle-faced man was the third U.S. president. He was born on April 13, 1743, on an estate in western Virginia. His father was a frontier planter and surveyor. He had a daughter named Martha. Interestingly, this president was a gifted inventor. He was self-conscious about his red hair. He invented a hide-away bed, a revolving music stand, and a walking stick that unfolded into a chair. He suffered many bad headaches.

II.

Suppose you are going to write a paragraph about Amelia Earhart, the famous flyer. Before you begin, you will need to get some information about her life. Probably, you will go to the library and look into an encyclopedia.

The following entry is from *The World Book Encyclopedia.* Underline the facts and the details that you would use in a paragraph about Amelia Earhart. Underline only those items that seem most important or interesting. One fact has been underlined for you.

EARHART, AMELIA (1897–1937?), became the first woman to cross the Atlantic Ocean by air and the first woman to fly it alone. She was also the first woman to receive the Distinguished Flying Cross.

Earhart was born at Atchison, Kans. She studied at Columbia University after nursing wounded soldiers during World War I. But she dropped out of school and worked in California to earn money for flying lessons. She worked briefly in Boston as a social worker.

In 1928, Earhart became the first female passenger on a transatlantic flight. She flew from Newfoundland to Burry Port, Wales. She wrote a book about this experience and later married her publisher, George Putnam. In 1932, Earhart flew across the Atlantic Ocean alone, from Harbour Grace, Newfoundland, to Ireland. She was the first woman to fly from Honolulu to the U.S. mainland and the first to fly across the United States alone in both directions. In 1937, she tried to fly

around the world. Her plane vanished near Howland Island in the Pacific Ocean, and no trace of Earhart or her plane was ever found by searchers.

ROBERT B. HOTZ

Getting Ready to Write

Soon you are going to go behind the history curtain. You are going to describe a famous person without giving the person's name. The following activities will get you ready to write.

I.

Circle the name of *one* of the famous people listed below about whom you would like to know more (and about whom you'd like to write). You may add a name of your own choice to the list by writing it on the line provided.

Pancho Villa   Alexander Graham Bell   Queen Victoria   Marie Curie   Clara Barton

Susan B. Anthony   Theodore Roosevelt   Martin Luther King, Jr.   Agatha Christie

Gwendolyn Brooks   Mary, Queen of Scots   Jim Morrison   Jimi Hendrix

Roberto Clemente   Jim Thorpe   Josip Broz Tito   John F. Kennedy   Emily Dickinson

Bill Cosby   Helen Keller   Hernando Cortez   _____

II.

In an encyclopedia, a magazine, or another source of information, look up the person whose name you either circled or wrote on the line in Part I. Then, on a separate sheet of paper, list *in your own words* the most important and interesting facts you find about this person. At the end of your list, write the title(s) of the source(s) you used.

Writing about History Makers

On a separate sheet of paper, write a description of the famous person you chose in Part I of "Getting Ready to Write" (page 15). Do not give the name of the person in your paragraph. However, *do* choose facts and details carefully so that your reader will be able to figure out who it is you are describing. Use the list of facts you made in "Getting Ready to Write," Part II, as a guide.

SKILL BUILDING

Capitalization and End Punctuation

You know that every sentence begins with a capital letter and ends with a punctuation mark.

> 1. A period (.) is used at the end of a sentence that makes a statement or a request or gives an ordinary command:
> Diana Ross and two friends formed a singing group in 1958.
> Please bring me the Diana Ross record.
> Bring the record over here.
> 2. A question mark (?) is used at the end of a sentence that asks a question:
> Was Diana Ross born in Detroit, Michigan, in 1944?
> 3. An exclamation point (!) is used at the end of a sentence that expresses a strong feeling or gives a forceful command:
> Wow! Diana Ross's new album is great!
> Turn that radio down!

I.

There are two sentences in each of the following items. Write the correct punctuation mark at the end of each sentence. The first item has been done for you.

1. It's amazing!   Does Sammy Davis, Jr. really earn three million dollars a year?

2. Is Alice Cooper's real name Vincent D. Furnier   A friend told me that it is

3. Cesar Chávez's parents could earn only 50¢ a day picking peas   That's terrible

4. Roberta Flack was once a teacher   That's amazing

5. Did I tell you about Dustin Hoffman   He once worked typing entries for the Yellow Pages

6. Was Michael Jackson's father a crane operator   I didn't know that

II.

The following paragraph describes the teenage years of Lyndon Johnson, the 36th U.S. president. All the capital letters and end-punctuation marks have been left out. Add capital letters and end marks where they are needed. Before you begin, review *proper nouns* on page 10. The first capital letter has been added for you.

What was lyndon baines johnson like as a teenager at the age of 15 he graduated from johnson city high school lyndon's mother urged him to go on to college did he do as she wished absolutely not instead of going to college he ran away with some friends to california there lyndon picked fruit, washed dishes, and did other odd jobs finally he made his way back to johnson city he decided that he would give college a try he enrolled at southwest texas state teachers college in san marcos he graduated at the age of 22 the rest is history

THINKING ABOUT WRITING

1. Give to a classmate the history-maker description you wrote. Ask your classmate to figure out who the person is that you have described.

2. Ask your classmate if too few or too many details are given in your description. Talk about details that can be crossed out—details that are uninteresting or that give no useful information. If your classmate cannot name the person described, talk about details that may be added.

3. On your paper, copy the *one* sentence that you and your classmate feel gives the best clue to the identity of the person you have described.

4. On your paper, copy the *one* sentence that you and your classmate feel gives the most interesting fact or detail.

SKILL BUILDING

5. Have you capitalized all proper nouns and the first word of every sentence? Make any corrections that are needed.

6. Be sure that you have used periods, question marks, and exclamation points correctly.

STORY WRITING MADE EASY

Many people think that story writing is hard. Some say they don't know what to write about. Others say they can't get started. And even if they do get a story started—and perhaps even finish it—it doesn't sound the way they had hoped it would.

In this lesson there will be some strange goings-on. You will read and write and think about impossible things. There's a reason for this. Through all the odd happenings, you will find out how easy it can be to write a story.

As a matter of fact, let's start with one of the "easiest" stories ever written.

The Story

Was I sore when I got home from school yesterday! Our English teacher told us to write a story. I asked her what we were supposed to write about. She said, "Oh, just use your imagination."

But I don't have any imagination. After dinner I sat in front of our typewriter in the den. For hours I tried to think of a story. Nothing, absolutely nothing, was happening. I made a few false starts, but nothing I wrote was any good.

Finally, my mom came in and said I had to go to bed. But I told her I couldn't. I had to write my story, and it surely wasn't going to write itself.

Guess who won the argument? My mom did, as usual. And off I went, up the stairs to bed, leaving a blank sheet of paper in the typewriter. I fell asleep thinking of the big fat *F* I was going to get in English the next day.

In the middle of the night, I suddenly woke up. The house was very dark and still, but I could hear a funny noise. Downstairs, someone was typing. It was my mom, I was sure. She was writing my story for me.

I went down the stairs toward the den. The typing got louder and louder. I flipped on the den light, in the same instant wondering why Mom would be typing in the dark. Then I just stared in disbelief. The typewriter was typing, but Mom wasn't there! No one was there! It was going all by itself!

Then it stopped. I pulled out what the machine had written. It was a story— the story I needed for my English class. I had been saved by my typewriter!

You may be wondering what my story was about. The truth is, you already know. You just read it.

THINKING ABOUT WHAT YOU HAVE READ

Answer in complete sentences.

1. What is the main character's problem? Explain the problem and tell how it is solved.

   _____

   _____

2. Have you ever faced a problem like the one faced by the person telling the story? Have you ever been asked to write something that caused you a lot of trouble? Explain your answer.

   _____

   _____

   _____

3. *Plot* is made up of the main events that happen in a story. What do you think are the most important things that happen in "The Story"?

   _____

   _____

4. The last paragraph of "The Story" has a surprise. What is the surprise?

   _____

   _____

THINKING ABOUT WRITING

Plot

The *plot* of a story is a sequence, or an order, of connected events. These events are the framework of the story. They move the story toward its ending. For example, the following events, in sequence, make up a story plot.

1. A girl goes into a cemetery that is said to be full of ghosts.
2. The girl talks to the caretaker of the cemetery. The caretaker laughs and assures her that there are no ghosts there.
3. After she leaves, she finds out that the caretaker died two years earlier.

I.

The events in each of the following lists are parts of a story plot. But the events are out of order. Number the events in the correct order to form a plot that makes sense. Two events in list 1 are numbered for you.

1. _____ **a.** He buys a car, even though the payments will be very large.

   ___1___ **b.** A guy asks a girl for a date for the following Saturday, and she accepts.

   _____ **c.** The girl drops the guy for someone else—a guy who doesn't have his own car.

   _____ **d.** He goes out with the girl. They like each other and start going around together.

   _____ **e.** After a while, the guy takes a night job to pay for the car. They can't go out very often, so the girl gets bored with him.

   ___2___ **f.** The guy doesn't have a car. He decides he has to get one before the date on Saturday. He figures that the girl will think he's a nobody if he has no car.

2. _____ **a.** A boy has very curly hair, which he hates. He makes a shampoo that he thinks will straighten his hair for life.

   _____ **b.** After a few weeks of baldness, the boy's head begins to sprout new curly hair. Soon he has a full head of curly hair. He's very happy to have his hair back.

   _____ **c.** The new shampoo makes his hair stop growing longer, but it also makes his hair become shorter. It shrinks down to nothing, and the boy is bald.

   _____ **d.** He rubs the shampoo into his hair. His hair goes straight, but it also begins growing at a rate of three inches a second.

   _____ **e.** The boy makes a new shampoo, one that will make his hair stop growing.

II.

Read the following story. As you do, think about the plot. That is, decide which events seem to be the most important, and keep those events in mind. You will be asked to outline the plot when you have finished reading.

The Man in the Glass Bubble

The crew of the Foster and Meyer Construction Company was digging a foundation for a 300-story building in Menlo Park, New Jersey.

One day Harlan Moore, one of the workers, stuck his shovel into the dirt. Nothing was there. The shovel went right through the dirt, leaving a jagged hole at Harlan's feet. Harlan called the other workers, and they came running.

Harlan got down on his stomach and looked through the hole. He could tell that there was a cave or something like it below him, but it was too dark to see. Harlan lit a match. That didn't help at all, so one of the other workers ran and got a large flashlight.

With the flashlight, Harlan could see something round and shiny in the middle of a cave. Excited, he got a rope and tied it to a tractor. Then he knotted the rope and slowly began to climb down into the hole. Soon he landed with a big PLOP on the dusty floor of the cave.

Brushing himself off, Harlan got up and searched the cave with his flashlight. In the center of the cave was a big glass bubble, or dome. Harlan gasped. Inside the dome was an old man! The man looked as though he were alive. But his eyes were closed, and he was neither moving nor breathing. Also, he was wearing very old-fashioned clothes—and he looked familiar, like someone Harlan had seen in history books. Stepping closer, Harlan could hear a humming sound. He could see that the dome was on some sort of engine or machine. On the front of the machine was a button with the words *Push to End Cycle* above it.

His hand trembling, Harlan pushed the button.

Suddenly the man started breathing. His eyes opened. His head moved, and his eyes fixed on Harlan. The man smiled. He stood up.

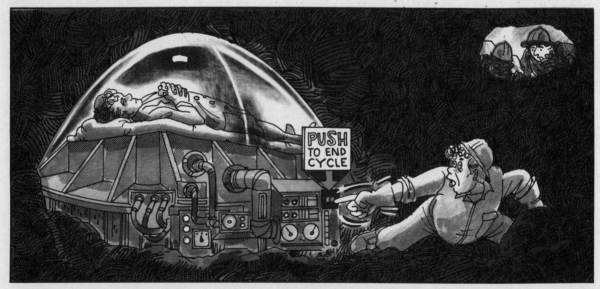

"It worked!" cried the man happily, as he stepped out of the bubble. "Please," he said, touching Harlan's arm as if to reassure him. "Please allow me to explain. You see, in 1931—almost 70 years ago—I invented my life-storage machine. But people weren't ready for it. To prove that it could work, I decided to test it on myself. I brought it down here to this cave, got in, and turned it on. Not until you pushed the button and ended the cycle had I been aware of a thing."

For a long moment the old man looked at Harlan. Seeing that his listener was confused and at a loss for words, the man went on with his story.

"In 1931 I was supposed to have died. A funeral with an empty coffin was arranged. That allowed me to try out my machine without interference."

Suddenly, Harlan realized who the man was. He was a man whose picture Harlan had seen in history books many times—a man who had been one of the greatest inventors of all time—a man who was supposed to have been dead over half a century. Harlan gasped. The man was . . .

"Allow me to introduce myself," said the man. "Edison's the name. Thomas Edison."

On the lines that follow, outline the plot of "The Man in the Glass Bubble." List in order the most important events that happen in the story. The first one has been listed for you.

(Remember that the plot does not include *every* detail found in the story. It includes only the *main* events. If your list has more than six to eight events, you have written too many. Go back and cross out all but the most important things that happen if your finished list includes more than eight events.)

1. *A worker named Harlan Moore digs a hole that cuts through the roof of a cave.*

Getting Ready to Write

The opening story in this unit was about someone who had to write a story but couldn't. Everything was taken care of when the typewriter developed a mind of its own and wrote the story itself. "The Story" (pages 18–19) follows a pattern often used in telling stories. That is, the main character is faced with a problem. The reader wonders how this problem will be worked out. The *climax*—or high point near the end—comes when a solution is found.

Soon you are going to write a story in which there is some sort of problem. As in "The Story," the problem will be worked out by a thing. The following activities will give you the outline for your story.

I.

At the left are problems. At the right are solutions provided by machines and other things. Carefully read each problem and each solution. Then match each numbered problem with the letter of the best solution.

		PROBLEMS		*SOLUTIONS*

PROBLEMS

_____ 1. You need to vacuum every room in a large house, but you are tired and the job is too big.

_____ 2. You are driving across a desert when you suddenly become ill—too ill to drive.

_____ 3. A dying woman wants to write her will, but she is too weak to do so.

_____ 4. A boy is trying to steal your boxing gloves.

_____ 5. A pioneer woman walking across the desert has no water left in her canteen.

SOLUTIONS

a. A pen picks itself up and writes the will.

b. The gloves put up a good fight and knock the boy down.

c. The canteen begins filling itself.

d. Your car drives you home by itself.

e. The vacuum cleaner starts itself up and vacuums the whole house.

II.

Follow the two steps given below.

1. Choose *one* of the problem–solution pairs you matched in Part I. It will be the basis of the story you are going to write.

2. Now that you know how your story will begin (with the problem) and end (with the solution), you need to know what will happen in between. That is, you need a plot. On the following lines, list in order the most important events that will happen in your story. Try to limit the list to three or four events.

_____

_____

_____

_____

_____

Story Writing

Above, you chose a story idea—a problem and a solution. Then you plotted the story. On a separate sheet of paper, write your story. Use your answers to "Getting Ready to Write," Part II, to guide you.

SKILL BUILDING

Capitalization and End Punctuation

You know that every sentence begins with a capital letter. Proper nouns—the names of particular persons, places, and things—are also capitalized. (For a review of proper nouns, turn to page 10.) The pronoun *I* is always written as a capital letter.

You've also learned that every sentence ends with a punctuation mark. A question mark (**?**) is used at the end of a sentence that asks a question. An exclamation point (**!**) is used at the end of a sentence that shows strong feeling. All other sentences end with a period (**.**).

Capital letters and end-of-sentence punctuation marks are missing from the following story. Add the capital letters and the punctuation marks where they are needed.

Martian Radio

i got a letter one day it was from a lawyer the letter said that my cousin bertha had a little problem she was saying that martians were talking to her through her radio according to the letter, she was sent off to an asylum as a result, her house now belonged to yours truly

lickety-split, i moved into the house it had a nice garden for growing things and a couple of cows that i could milk boy, i thought i had it made

then it happened that one day i turned on bertha's old radio sure enough, a martian was talking to me he wanted me to come to mars to visit him

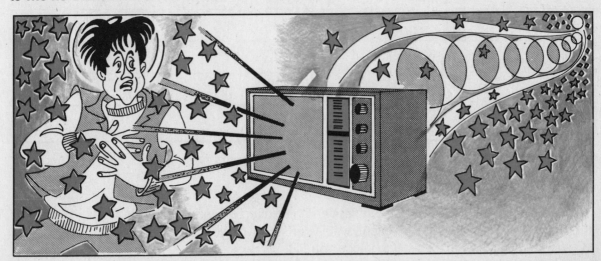

of course, i told everybody about the martian i also told them that bertha wasn't goofy i told them flat out that a martian rascal really did talk through her radio

well, things just got worse for poor old me the whole town thought i was nuts yes, you guessed it i'm now off for a long rest with bertha it's very depressing we both tell the doctors that we didn't imagine all this, but they just shake their heads and look at us real sadly

last i heard elizabeth ann wickensogger, my niece, now has bertha's place i pity the poor girl i surely hope she doesn't ever turn on that radio if she does, i do expect her to be joining bertha and me before too long

THINKING ABOUT WRITING

1. Before you write a story, you outline a plot. But very often your story changes as you write. It takes a direction slightly different from your original plot line. Did this happen when you wrote your story for this lesson? If so, explain on a separate sheet of paper how your final story differs from your original plan.

2. Study the word order in five sentences in your story. On your paper, rewrite each of the five sentences, using the same words in a different word order. You may change statements into questions.

3. Are there any unnecessary sentences in your story? That is, are there any sentences that are uninteresting or give no useful information? If so, cross them out.

SKILL BUILDING

4. On your paper, list five common nouns from your story.

5. List on your paper the proper nouns you used in your story.

6. Check the capitalization and end-of-sentence punctuation in your story. Correct any errors you find.

SUMMING UP

A group of students in Hannibal, Missouri, was asked to read the following true story of a seemingly impossible event. Then they were asked to write summaries of it. (A *summary* gives the main points of something written or talked about at length.)

First, read the story yourself. Then go on to the summaries.

A Battle Won by Toy Soldiers

By far the strangest battle of all time may have been the one that was won by an army of toy soldiers. It all began with a man named Decebalus. Decebalus was the king of Dacia (now Romania) during the late first and early second centuries A.D. An able leader, Decebalus was also a collector of puppet soldiers. He had hundreds of them. All were life-sized and dressed like the troops of Dacia.

One day Decebalus received news that a Roman army was marching on Sarmizegethusa, the capital of Dacia. The soldiers and townspeople knew they were facing a much stronger force. Terrified, they awaited death at the hands of the Romans.

Suddenly Decebalus had an idea. As the Romans came into view across a distant plain, Decebalus ordered that all his toy soldiers be gathered and brought to him. The people were not sure what their king had in mind. Still, they did as they were told.

Decebalus told the people to tie ropes to the puppets and lower them over the city wall. Then he showed how to move the puppets about on the ground.

The Romans saw the huge toy army from a distance. They were scared. They thought they were greatly outnumbered. Everywhere they looked there were soldiers moving about beneath the city walls, preparing for battle.

If they had advanced a few hundred yards closer, the Romans would have discovered the trick that was being played on them. Instead, fearing for their lives, they turned on their heels and beat a hasty retreat.

Adding insult to injury, Decebalus followed up his victory by sending a note to Rome demanding money! The note said his "army" would attack and destroy Rome unless tribute was paid. The Romans did not realize they were being played for fools. They agreed to the demand. For the next ten years they paid an annual tribute to Dacia!

Now study two students' summaries of the story.

1. The Romans were invading. Decebalus didn't know what to do. He was the king, the king of Dacia. It was in the second century. Dacia is now Romania. So he got all the puppets together. The Romans attacked him, and they attacked his capital city. Decebalus used his puppets to beat the Romans.

2. A king named Decebalus once won a battle using toy soldiers. Decebalus's hobby was collecting life-sized puppet soldiers. One day the Roman army came to attack the king's town, and he did not have enough soldiers. Decebalus had an idea. He dangled all his puppets over the town wall. They were moved around like real soldiers. The Romans thought they were up against a huge army, and they ran away.

THINKING ABOUT WHAT YOU HAVE READ

Answer in complete sentences.

1. Do you think the story "A Battle Won by Toy Soldiers" is interesting? Explain your answer.

_____

_____

2. Which of the two summaries do you feel is the weaker? Give reasons for your answer.

_____

_____

3. Now study the other summary. List the reasons why you think this is a better summary.

_____

_____

THINKING ABOUT WRITING

Summary Paragraphs

A **summary paragraph** gives just the main points of something written or spoken at length. The topic sentence of a summary paragraph tells what the longer selection is about. For example, notice how the topic sentence of summary paragraph 2 on page 27 states the main idea of "A Battle Won by Toy Soldiers":

A king named Decebalus once won a battle using toy soldiers.

The rest of the sentences includes only the most important events and details—usually the *who, what, where, when, how,* and *why* of the story. In a good summary paragraph, these facts and details are given in a logical order that will make sense to the reader.

The selection that follows tells a true story. Read it carefully before going on.

The Last of His People

It was the morning of August 30, 1911. All the newspapers told the same shocking story. A "caveman" had been captured in Oroville, California!

The man had been found hiding behind a fence. He was naked except for a piece of cloth over his shoulders. There were leather thongs hanging from his ears and a wooden plug in his nose. He did not speak.

The sheriff put him in a jail cell. Many people came to peek through the window. They all wanted to see what was believed to be a prehistoric man.

A scientist named Waterman read the news story. He was very interested. He went to Oroville to find out more about the so-called caveman.

The sheriff let Waterman into the cell. Waterman realized that the man was really a Native American. He was a Yana. The Yanas were a Stone Age people that everyone thought was extinct.

Waterman spoke to the man in the Yana tongue. The silent man answered! He was very surprised and happy that someone could speak his language.

The Yana did not give his name. Waterman began calling him Ishi. The word means "man" in Yana.

Waterman took Ishi to San Francisco. There Ishi lived in a museum. He and Waterman became good friends. Ishi told Waterman the story of his life.

His people were poor and primitive, Ishi said. They lived by hunting, gathering, and fishing. Then the white men came. They killed the Yanas by the hundreds. The few Yanas who were left went into the hills to hide. But they too died, mostly from sickness and starvation. Finally, Ishi was the only one left. Not knowing where else to go, he decided to enter the white man's world.

In San Francisco some people treated Ishi very stupidly. A circus owner wanted to put him in a sideshow as a freak. A record company wanted him to sing. A producer asked him to come to Hollywood to become an actor.

Ishi wanted to stay at the museum. He learned English, and he was given a job as a janitor at a college. He learned to handle his own money. He shopped for himself and cooked his own food.

Sometimes Ishi worked as a teacher at the museum. He would talk about Yana culture. He would explain how his people hunted, how they cooked, and how they made shelters. He made baskets, spears, and bows and arrows. These were added to the museum collections. Sometimes as many as 1,000 people a day would come to the museum to see Ishi and the things he had made.

In 1915 Ishi fell sick. He slowly got worse. Doctors found he had tuberculosis. He lived one more year. He died on March 25, 1916. He was 54 years old.

Ishi was the last of the Yanas. And with his death, they too died—but not completely. During his last years he was able to show us their way of life. He was able to show us what the first true Americans were like.

I.

Underline the events and the details in "The Last of His People" that you would include in a summary paragraph. Make your choices carefully.

II.

The following are several events in the story about Ishi. Number them in *chronological* order—the order in which they happened. You would present the events in this order in a summary paragraph.

_____ **a.** Ishi lived and worked in a museum in San Francisco.

_____ **b.** Waterman took Ishi to San Francisco.

_____ **c.** Ishi died of tuberculosis.

_____ **d.** Ishi was captured in Oroville, California.

_____ **e.** Waterman went to Oroville.

_____ **f.** Ishi was put in a jail cell.

III.

The following are three possible topic sentences for a summary of "The Last of His People." Choose the *one* you think is most effective. Circle its number. Then, on a separate sheet of paper, explain your choice.

1. Ishi was a caveman who once lived in a museum in San Francisco.

2. "The Last of His People" is a story about the hardships suffered by the Yanas and about an Indian named Ishi.

3. "The Last of His People" is the true story of Ishi, the last surviving member of a Native American tribe.

Getting Ready to Write

Soon you are going to write a summary of the following true story. Begin by reading the selection. Then move on to the activities after it.

The Almost-King of the United States

You probably have never heard of Prince Henry of Germany. Few people have, for Prince Henry was a strange man who had little effect on the course of history.

There is only one interesting thing about the life of this individual. Believe it or not, he almost became King Henry I of the United States!

It happened this way.

By 1786 the American colonies had won their independence from England. The nation needed a ruler, but no one knew who this person should be. The debate had gone on and on.

In 1786 the question remained unsettled. Thus, in that year a powerful group of politicians got together. Included in the group were James Monroe, Alexander Hamilton, and Nathaniel Gortham, president of the Continental Congress. After a long discussion, the group members decided that what the United States needed was a king. And this king, they concluded, should come from one of the ruling families in Europe.

After more debate, they decided that Prince Henry of Germany, the younger brother of Frederick the Great, was the best man for the job. A few days later they sent a letter to Henry. They asked him to come to North America and become king of the United States.

Prince Henry was tempted to take the offer. But he could not make up his mind. Months went by, and he still had not made a decision. Americans got tired of waiting for his answer. The discussions continued. It was finally agreed that the country should have an elected president, not a king. The rest is history.

But what if Prince Henry had said yes to the offer? Had he done so, much of United States history might have been changed. Today, instead of an elected president, the nation might have a king or a queen, the descendant of a now-forgotten German prince who took too long to make up his mind.

I.

Go back to the selection "The Almost-King of the United States." Underline the details and the events that you would include in a summary paragraph.

II.

On the following lines, write a topic sentence for a summary paragraph for "The Almost-King of the United States."

_____

_____

_____

Writing a Summary Paragraph

On a separate sheet of paper, write a summary of "The Almost-King of the United States." Use your answers to "Getting Ready to Write" (page 30) to guide you.

SKILL BUILDING

Conjunctions and Run-on Sentences

Conjunctions join words and parts of sentences together. The following are the most common conjunctions:

and   but   or   yet   then   because   so

Conjunctions can cause problems for a writer. If they are used in the wrong way, run-on sentences are the result. **Run-on sentences** do not end as they should, with a single complete thought. They keep going on and on, using words such as *and, so, but,* and *then* to run many different ideas together.

In the following run-on sentence, the writer uses the conjunction *but* to join two different, complete thoughts. Notice how the sentence is corrected. The conjunction is replaced by a period. Then the second sentence starts with a capital letter.

(run-on):   Hetty Green was one of the strangest women in history but though terribly rich, she lived like a pauper her whole life.
(correct):   Hetty Green was one of the strangest women in history. ~~but~~ Though terribly rich, she lived like a pauper her whole life.

Correct the run-on sentences in each paragraph that follows. Cross out conjunctions that are not needed. Place punctuation marks at the end of sentences. Add capital letters where necessary. The first run-on sentence has been corrected for you.

1.   Electric lights were put into the White House during the presidency of Benjamin Harrison. ~~and~~ President Harrison and his wife, however, were so afraid of the newfangled device that they refused to touch the switches so the task of switch flipping was left to servants but when servants were not around the Harrisons slept with the lights burning.

2. In 1963 a puzzling incident occurred because in that year a group of Russian scientists reported that they had found two 5,000-year-old lizards and had brought them back to life because the lizards were found buried 25 feet (7.62 meters) in ice and frozen solid and they had been "dead" for thousands of years and the scientists let them thaw out at room temperature and gradually the creatures began to breathe and then they began to walk around!

3. Adolf Hitler was a draft dodger because in May 1913, to avoid being drafted into the Austrian army, he slipped across the border into Germany then he was arrested and returned to Austria and the Austrian officials told young Hitler that he would not go to jail if he joined the army so Hitler agreed to this condition, but he failed his physical exam.

4. In 1801 President Jefferson found that no one wanted to become Secretary of the Navy and he was at a loss to fill the position so he ran a "help-wanted" ad in newspapers then a man named Robert Smith answered his ad and was made Secretary of the Navy and Smith served from 1802 to 1805.

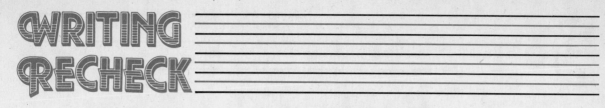
THINKING ABOUT WRITING

1. Underline the topic sentence of your summary paragraph on "The Almost-King of the United States." Does it tell what the whole story is about? If not, write a new topic sentence on a separate sheet of paper.

2. Have a classmate check the word order in your sentences. On your paper, rewrite any sentences whose word order your classmate feels can be improved.

3. Does your summary present the facts and details in an order that makes sense? Are events told in the order in which they happened? If order is the weak point of your paragraph, list the details and events you want to write about on a separate sheet of paper. Try rearranging the items until you have an order that you like. Then use the list as a guide in rewriting the paragraph.

SKILL BUILDING

4. Put a check mark (√) beside any of the following errors you find in your summary paragraph.

_____ failure to capitalize the first word of a sentence

_____ failure to capitalize proper nouns and the pronoun *I*

_____ end-of-sentence punctuation not used where needed

_____ run-on sentences

Make the necessary corrections.

TIME TRIP

We asked some students in Minneapolis, Minnesota, to take an imaginary step backward or forward in time. Then we asked them to write about their time trips. . . .

I have gone backward into prehistoric times. There are all sorts of strange animals. There are flying lizards, huge bats, and saber-toothed tigers. The people are ugly and short and hairy. They live by eating fruit and berries. They also hunt animals for food. The meat is always eaten raw. The cave people do not know how to make fire or how to cook.

Jennifer Robles

I have leapt through time into the year 2247. The earth is ruled by Mogoites. Mogoites are orange giants from the planet Mogo. In 2131 the Mogoites came in spaceships and conquered the earth. At first they were cruel and used humans only as servants. But in 2148 there was a revolution, and humans demanded equal rights. Now humans and Mogoites live and work side by side. They really don't like each other, but they get along fairly well.

Randy Tully

I am on Columbus's ship, the *Santa Maria.* All around there is nothing but blue-green water. Columbus is talking to another sailor. The things he is saying are interesting. He says he is on his way to India. He is also saying he does not think the world is round! He thinks it is shaped like a pear. Another of his beliefs is that ships sail uphill when they go west. He says his ships are rising higher in the sky. Soon he will reach India—the highest place on earth.

Michael Nordensen

I am in ancient Greece. A man is on trial for treason. The trial is very strange. It is being held at the beach. The man is in a boat that is placed offshore—as is the custom. A person accused of treason is always tried while in a boat. They think that the person will pollute the country if he or she sets foot in it. The man in the boat has to prove he is loyal and is not guilty. Only then can he step back on the land.

Sophie Washington

THINKING ABOUT WHAT YOU HAVE READ

Answer in complete sentences.

1. Jennifer Robles describes prehistoric people. What does she say prehistoric people look like?

_____

2. Randy Tully describes what the future might be like. How are details used to add interest to the paragraph? Give examples to support your answer.

_____

_____

_____

3. Sophie Washington's paragraph is based on fact. In your opinion, does basing a paragraph on this kind of historical fact make it more or less interesting? Explain why.

_____

_____

4. Imagine you are a teacher. You have just read all the student paragraphs on pages 34–35. First, give each one a grade (A, B, C, D, F). Then pick any one of the paragraphs and explain why you gave it the grade you did.

_____

_____

ᛟHINKING ᚨBOUT ᚹRITING

Redundant Writing

Do you like hearing the same thing over and over? If not, the following sentence will probably annoy you.

Prehistoric cave people had an average life span of about 20 years on the average.

Several words and ideas in the sentence are repeated. The word *cave* repeats an idea already made clear by the word *prehistoric*. The phrase *on the average* also is not needed. It restates an idea already conveyed by the words *had an average life span*. Writing in which words and ideas are repeated unnecessarily is said to be **redundant**.

Notice how the sentence is improved by removing these redundant words and phrases.

Prehistoric people had an average life span of about 20 years.

Cross out all the unnecessary words in each item that follows.

EXAMPLE: Prehistoric ~~cave~~ people lived for an average of ~~about~~ 20 years.
~~on the average.~~

1. Previously basketball before now was once played with eight players on each team.

2. Thomas Edison never went further than the first grade in school because his teachers thought and believed he was "strange and stupid" and shouldn't go any further.

3. The Babylonians treated the sickness we today call leprosy by soaking the diseased areas and parts of the body in beer.

4. George Washington's favorite dish was cream of peanut soup, which he liked best.

5. The soldiers of old ancient Rome and Greece had make-believe battles that resembled and were like the game of football.

6. In the olden days in the 1400s in Italy it was illegal and a crime for women to wear buttons.

7. During the Franco-Prussian War (1870–1871), the people of France were so hungry and were driven by starvation to eat the animals in the Paris Zoo during the war.

8. "The Star-Spangled Banner" has not been our national anthem all along because it did not become our national anthem until fairly recently in 1931.

9. Both Herbert Hoover, the 31st U.S. president, and Mao Tse-tung, the Chinese leader of China, were both librarians.

10. The first original name of Utah was Deseret; it wasn't Utah.

Getting Ready to Write

The following activity will help you get ready to write about an imaginary trip into the past or the future.

Follow the directions for each step.

1. Browse through a history book or an encyclopedia. On the lines, write the names of five people from the past you would like to meet. (Queen Victoria, for example)

   _____

   _____

2. List five events from the past you would like to see. (The Battle of Gettysburg, for example)

   _____

   _____

   _____

3. Now imagine you are going into the future. On the lines, list three things you think you might see. (People living in undersea cities, for example)

   _____

   _____

4. Reread what you have written for items 1 through 3 above. Which "time trip" would be most interesting for you? Which would you most like to write about? Write your choice on the following line.

   _____

5. You have decided where you're going in your "time-trip" paragraph. Now write a topic sentence for this paragraph. (Use the topic sentences of the paragraphs on pages 34 through 35 as models.)

   _____

   _____

Writing a "Time-Trip" Paragraph

On a separate sheet of paper, write your paragraph about a visit into either the past or the future. Use your answers to "Getting Ready to Write" to help you.

SKILL BUILDING

Verb Tense

Every sentence must have a verb. Most often, the verb tells what the subject of the sentence does, did, or will do. In the following sentences, the subject is underlined and the verb is circled.

Liza Minelli (sings) in the 1977 film *New York, New York*.

William ("Captain") Kidd once (defended) English ships against pirates.

We (will find) some famous facts.

The verb can also tell what the subject is, was, or will be.

Former pitcher Jim Bouton (is) the author of a best-selling book.

James Butler ("Wild Bill") Hickok (was) a Union scout during the Civil War.

Robots (will be) part of everyday life before very long.

I.

Add a verb to each sentence that follows by writing between the lines.

EXAMPLE: In 1930 astronomer C. Tombaugh ^*discovered* the planet Pluto.

1. We _____ up to 70 tons of food in an average lifetime.

2. King Henry VIII of England _____ a tennis player.

3. Alan Alda _____ in movies before the *M*A*S*H* series began.

4. Bill Cosby _____ to Temple University on a football scholarship.

5. New Yorkers _____ two million cups of coffee every 20 minutes.

6. Boris Karloff's real name _____ William Henry Pratt.

7. The Sahara Desert _____ once a tropical climate.

8. The U.S.S.R. _____ the first satellite into orbit around the earth.

9. Louis Chevrolet, Ransom Olds, and Henry Ford all cars after themselves.

10. As a child, Barbara Walters a career as a tap dancer.

Verbs not only show action or being. They also show time. Notice how the following sentence is changed from *present* time to *past* time to *future* time simply by changing the form of the verb *help*.

(present time): Cindy <u>helps</u> him.
Cindy and Joan <u>help</u> him.
(past time): Cindy <u>helped</u> him.
(future time): Cindy <u>will help</u> him.

II.

Pretend that the following statements were made by the famous persons pictured below. In the blank next to each person's name, write *past, present,* or *future* to indicate the time shown by the underlined verb.

1. _____ Florence Nightingale: "I <u>carry</u> a pet owl, even when I'm traveling."

2. _____ Ben Franklin: "I <u>invented</u> daylight saving time."

3. _____ Anne Boleyn: "In my time, I <u>was</u> a skilled archer."

4. _____ Martian: "In the year 1999 I <u>will visit</u> Earth."

5. _____ Stevie Wonder: "My real name <u>is</u> Steveland Morris."

A common mistake that writers make is to shift without reason from one time period and verb tense to another. That is, their use of verbs is not consistent. In the following example, the writer switches back and forth between past and present time.

I *am walking* through a forest. I *heard* the sound of gunfire. I *run* up a hill and *looked* down. In a valley below, General Lee *was leading* his troops toward a Yankee camp. Everybody *is yelling*.

Notice how the paragraph is improved by making all the verbs show the same time. Here, the writer has chosen past time for the paragraph.

I *was walking* through a forest. I *heard* the sound of gunfire. I *ran* up a hill and *looked* down. In a valley below, General Lee *was leading* his troops toward a Yankee camp. Everybody *was yelling*.

III.

Improve the selection that follows by making the verbs consistent. All the verbs should show past time. Make any changes that are needed.

In 1759 George Washington marries Martha Custis. If he had married someone else, the White

House would probably has a different name.

When George meets Martha she owns a plantation that had belonged to her first husband.

Martha's pet name for the place is "the White House."

The White House, today, in Washington, D.C.

In 1789 George Washington becomes the first president of the United States. A short time later a "presidential palace" is built. Washington calls it "the White House" in memory of the plantation house he and his wife had loved so much.

The original plantation "White House" is destroyed in the Civil War in 1861. Its last owner is Mrs. Robert E. Lee, a descendant of Martha Washington.

WRITING RECHECK

THINKING ABOUT WRITING

1. Study your "time-trip" paragraph. Is the topic sentence effective in giving the main idea? Does it let the reader know what your writing is about? If not, write a new topic sentence on a separate sheet of paper.

2. Did you repeat words or ideas in your paragraph? If so, cross out the redundant words and phrases.

3. Study the word order in your sentences. On your paper, rewrite any sentences in which the word order can be improved.

SKILL BUILDING

4. Reread your paragraph to see if you have made any of the following errors. Put a check mark (√) next to those that you find.

_____ failure to capitalize the first words of sentences

_____ failure to capitalize proper nouns or the pronoun *I*

_____ run-on sentences

_____ inconsistent verbs (shifting back and forth among different times)

Now correct your paragraph.

LOVE STORIES

Love is such an important part of life. Writers through the ages have written about it. They have tried, in many different ways, to explain what love is all about.

We asked a class in Los Angeles, California, to write some love stories. The story could be about a famous person. It could be a made-up story, or it could be a true story from the writer's life. Here is what three students wrote.

One person I'll always love is my dad. He is truly a wonderful man. He is always easygoing and cheerful and always has good things to say about other people. He is the kind of person who thinks more about other people than about himself. I can always go to him with my problems, and he is never too busy to listen. And after we talk, I always feel good. I know that somebody really understands me and cares about me and loves me.

Roger Thornton

Last year I was going with a boy named Mike. He meant everything to me, and I loved him. He said he loved me, too. But then I found out Mike was playing me for a fool. All along he had been seeing another girl, named Judy. Finally he broke up with me and started going with Judy. But it wasn't long before Judy started playing Mike for a fool, and then she broke up with him. A couple of weeks ago Mike called me up and said he wanted to see me again. I said no. It was a hard thing to do. But I had learned my lesson. I don't want a guy like Mike. I want someone who will be true and honest. Those are about the most important parts of love.

Ellen Racorskowitz

Marilyn Monroe's life is one of the saddest love stories ever. She was born Norma Jean Baker. She was always being sent away to boarding schools. Norma Jean was first married at the age of 16 to James Daughtery. The marriage lasted until Jim sailed off to fight in World War II. Norma Jean moved to Hollywood, became an actress, and changed her name to Marilyn Monroe. Her second marriage was to Joe DiMaggio, the baseball player. A few years later they were divorced. Then she married the writer Arthur Miller. In all of her marriages Marilyn was never really happy. She seemed to be a person who was always looking for love but could never find it.

Todd Sullivan

THINKING ABOUT WHAT YOU HAVE READ

Answer in complete sentences.

1. What happens in the love story by Ellen Racorskowitz?

_____

_____

_____

2. Which of the love stories do you think is the saddest? Explain why.

_____

_____

_____

3. Two of the stories are based on personal experience. Which are they? Explain how you are able to tell.

_____

_____

_____

4. Which of the stories is based on historical fact? Discuss the differences between this story and the others.

_____

_____

_____

THINKING ABOUT WRITING

Word Choice

Sometimes when you write you will find it hard to think of just the right word. As a result, you may use many carelessly chosen words to take the place of one word that can convey your meaning exactly.

In the following items, several words are used where one well-chosen word will do the job. Cross out the underlined words and replace them with a word from the list at the right.

painter.

EXAMPLE: He was married to a ~~person who does paintings~~

1. In Ruanda, Africa, the marriage ceremony consists of the <u>man who is going to be the husband</u> whitewashing his bride's face.

2. Dolly Parton's husband has never seen her <u>do her singing before a big audience.</u>

3. Burt Reynolds's first love was playing football. However, he had to quit when a serious knee injury <u>ruined and put a stop to</u> his career.

4. Erich Segal was a <u>college or university teacher</u> at Yale when he wrote *Love Story,* one of the most popular novels of the 1970s.

5. In Kashmir, India, the woman does not <u>go to or take part</u> in her own wedding. Instead, a camel is sent to represent her at the ceremony.

6. In 1964 a Masai chieftain made a strange marriage <u>suggestion or request.</u> He offered actress Carroll Baker 150 cows, 200 goats, and $750 in cash if she would marry him.

7. In 1978 Donna Summer married a <u>person who plays the guitar</u> named Bruce Sudano.

8. At the age of 19, Cheryl Tiegs married Stan Dragoti, a <u>person who directs movies.</u>

9. In ancient Rome unmarried girls were <u>not allowed</u> by law to wear pearls.

10. Elizabeth Taylor was once married to a <u>person who produces movies</u> named Michael Todd.

forbidden
groom
attend
producer
proposal
director
perform
guitarist
professor
ended

Getting Ready to Write

Soon you are going to write a "love story." The following activities will help you to get started.

I.

Imagine you are going to write a personal narrative about a love for some special person. Which of the following people will you write about? (Circle one, or write a choice of your own in the blank.)

mother   father   brother   sister   aunt   uncle   cousin   grandmother

grandfather   boyfriend   girlfriend   other _____

II.

Imagine you are going to write about the life and loves of a famous person. First, look up *one* of the persons listed below in an encyclopedia, almanac, or a nonfiction book about that person. On a separate sheet of paper, write five facts about the person's life. (You may add a choice of your own to the list by writing a name in the blank.)

Edgar Allan Poe   Henry VIII   Barbra Streisand   George Washington   U Thant

Diana Ross   Emily Dickinson   Queen Elizabeth I   Cleopatra   Napoleon Bonaparte

Carol Burnett   Woody Allen   O. J. Simpson   other _____

III.

A. Now imagine you are going to write a fictional, or made-up, love story. In the following list are some characters you might include in such a story. Circle *two* or *three* of the characters in the list. You may add other characters by writing on the line.

a child   an elderly woman (or man)   a doctor   a teenage boy who lives on a farm

a rich city girl   a patient in a hospital   a singer   a shy young man   an orphan

an elderly couple   a teenage girl _____

B. What sort of love story could you write about the characters you selected? On a separate sheet of paper, write a rough sketch of what might happen in a story about these people.

Writing Your Love Story

The "Getting Ready to Write" activities (page 45) asked you to think about the types of love stories you might write. Now decide which story you will actually write. You may write a personal narrative (Part I), a story about a famous person (Part II), or a fictional story (Part III).

When you've made your decision, write your love story on the lines below. Use your answers to "Getting Ready to Write" to guide you.

SKILL BUILDING

Pronouns

A **pronoun** is a word used in place of a noun. The following are some commonly used pronouns.

I   you   he   she   it   we   they   me   him   her
us   them   my   your   his   its   our   their

Notice how pronouns replace the underlined nouns in the following:

NOUNS	PRONOUNS
Danny came home.	He came home.
There's one in Mom's office.	There's one in her office.
No one brought napkins.	No one brought them.

I.

Each sentence that follows contains an underlined noun. By crossing out one or more letters in each noun, change it into a correct pronoun.

EXAMPLE: Hector was just standing there.

1. I can't see mother.

2. Sheila plans to go to college.

3. Knitting is her hobby.

4. Ask my father to help Romeo.

5. Cheryl's foot got caught.

6. That is Whistler's book.

7. Did Sheldon help at all?

8. We're the Bowers, and Bowers are tough.

What is the purpose of pronouns? For one thing, without them we would have to keep repeating the same nouns over and over again. For example, notice what happens when a sentence is written without using any pronouns: *David went to the store so that David could buy David's sister a present.*

II.

Cross out the underlined nouns in the following sentences and replace them with correct pronouns.

EXAMPLE: David went to the store so that ~~David~~ *he* could buy ~~David's~~ *his* sister a present.

1. Sally Field married the first man Sally Field ever dated.

2. Cleopatra married Cleopatra's own brother. This was a custom in Cleopatra's time.

3. Pygmy brides wear no shoes, so pygmy brides have shoelike designs painted on pygmy brides' legs and feet.

4. A farmer once fell in love with a girl the farmer saw in a dream. After searching for the girl for many months, the farmer actually found the girl!

5. In the 1600s a man named Zebi staged a wedding in which Zebi married Zebi's Bible.

THINKING ABOUT WRITING

1. Ask a classmate to read your love story (page 46) and give you a grade (A,B,C,D,F). Then, on a separate sheet of paper, have your classmate explain the reasons for the grade you were given.

2. Are there any instances in which you have used many words where one or two would have conveyed your meaning better? If so, correct this error wherever it occurs.

SKILL BUILDING

3. Place a check mark (√) beside any of the following errors you find in your love story.

    _____ failure to capitalize proper nouns

    _____ incorrect end-of-sentence punctuation

    _____ run-on sentences

    _____ repeated use of nouns where pronouns are needed

    _____ incorrect pronouns

    Now correct your story.

POETRY WRITING

We invited students in the San Fernando Valley of California to send us rhyming poems. The response was wonderful. On this and the following page, we have printed just a few of the poems we received.

When the Sun Goes Down

When the sun goes down
It means the night is near
When the sun goes down
It means darkness will appear
When the sun goes down

By David Jacobs

The Moon

The moon
Is what I want
Gift wrapped with
Ribbon not string
Beautifully set
On a stunning gold ring
If that I cannot have
Then give me the sea
With the silver moonlit reflection
Shining brightly at me
Those two gifts—
Most precious they are
But if you cannot give that
Then I must have the stars
The North Star
The brightest
The stars of Taurus
Bring them to me kneeling
Then I'll place them
On my ceiling
These are the only things
That I desire
Three simple gifts
That will never expire

By Wendy Abbey

Discovery

Today I smiled, and all at once,
Things didn't look quite so bad.
Today I shared with someone else,
A bit of hope I had.
Today I sang part of a song,
And felt my heart grow light,
And walked down a carefree mile,
With not a cloud in sight.
Today I worked with what I had,
Not longed for any more,
And what had seemed like only weeds,
Were roses at my door.
Today I loved a little more,
And complained a little less,
And in this giving of myself,
Forgot my weariness. . . .

By Anthony Garcia

They Fly Without Haste

They fly without haste
through the galaxies of space
throughout the universe they fly
in search of a telescopic eye
faster than the speed of light
in a timeless zone of flight
A comet strikes around the bend
the impossible journey will never end

By David Gonzales

Time

Time steps by me quickly
Stepping by quietly.
I tried to catch some in my hand
But yet it always breaks free
All I can do is let time be. . . .

By Ari Davidson

Silent Sea

Silent sea
White dawn of dreams
Shadows lost in
Blue pasture
Bleeding streams.
Liquid nights pure
In brilliance,
        masterfully refined.
Cold in slumber,
The forest lumber.
The scowl crowns the lion's hide
    sleep my child
Close your eyes
Your prison skies
The ancient Satyr's poem
resides.
The day is awakening
From the monstrous skin
The waves arise from
The battered wind
    Who will win?
    Who will win?

By Anthony Mendoza

THINKING ABOUT WHAT YOU HAVE READ

Answer in complete sentences.

1. What is Anthony Garcia saying in his poem? What idea is he trying to get across? Explain your answer.

   _____

   _____

   _____

2. What is Ari Davidson saying about time? Do you agree? Explain why or why not.

   _____

   _____

   _____

3. Which of the poems do you enjoy least? Explain why.

   _____

   _____

   _____

   _____

4. Which of the poems do you feel is the best? Explain why.

   _____

   _____

   _____

   _____

5. Do you find Anthony Mendoza's poem difficult or easy to understand? Give reasons for your answer.

   _____

   _____

   _____

   _____

THINKING ABOUT WRITING

Understanding Rhyme in Poems

People sometimes ask whether poetry must always rhyme. The answer is no—all poetry does not rhyme. A poem may be written with or without rhyme. However, rhyme is often used by many people who write poems.

The rhyming words at the ends of lines of poetry often follow a pattern. This pattern is called a *rhyme scheme.* Letters of the alphabet can be used to show the rhyme scheme of most poems. Each ending sound is given a letter, starting with *A.* Any words that rhyme are given the same letter, as you see in the following example.

Little Jack Horner   *a*

Sat in a corner   *a*

Eating a Christmas pie   *B*

He stuck in his thumb   *C*

And pulled out a plum   *C*

And said, "What a good boy am I!"   *B*

Write letters in the blanks to show the rhyme scheme of each poem that follows. Use the example poem ("Little Jack Horner") as a guide. Remember: Any words that rhyme get the same letter. Words that don't yet rhyme with anything get a new letter.

1. 'Tis late to hearken, late to smile,   _____

   But better late than never;   _____

   I shall have lived a little while   _____

   Before I die forever.   _____
           By A. E. Housman

2. Up into the cherry tree   _____

   Who should climb but little me?   _____

   I held the trunk with both my hands   _____

   And looked abroad on foreign lands.   _____
           By R. L. Stevenson

52

3. A child should always say what's true, _____

And speak when he is spoken to, _____

And behave mannerly at table, _____

At least as far as he is able. _____
By R. L. Stevenson

4. A burro once, sent by express _____

His shipping ticket on his bridle _____

Ate up his name and his address, _____

And in some warehouse, standing idle, _____

He waited till he like to died. _____

The moral hardly needs the showing: _____

Don't keep things locked up inside, _____

Say who you are and where you're going. _____
By Walker Gibson

Getting Ready to Write

On pages 54 and 55 you are going to write some rhyming poems. The following activities will help you get ready to write.

1. For each word given, write five words that rhyme. Do your work on a separate sheet of paper.

   a. man   **b.** bite   **c.** west   **d.** slide   **e.** spilling

2. Two short rhymes follow. Decide which sounds better. Then, on your paper, tell which rhyme you chose, and give the reasons for your choice.

   a. There was a genie
      Who was really a terrible and awful and nasty meanie

   b. There was a genie
      Who was such a meanie

Writing Rhyming Poetry

Now it's time to write some rhyming poetry of your own. Write poems on the lines provided, using the given words as the rhymes. Begin each line with a capital letter.

EXAMPLE:
I know a boy named Billy
Who always acts so silly
He wears his clothes upside down
And paints his face like a clown

1. _____ Sue
   _____ blue
   _____ away
   _____ day

2. _____ car
   _____ star
   _____ air
   _____ care

The rhyming poems you just wrote have an AABB rhyme scheme. The first two lines rhyme, as do the last two. Your next poems will have an ABAB rhyme scheme. In these poems every other line will rhyme.

3. _____ street
   _____ be
   _____ beat
   _____ free

4. _____ wrong
   _____ button
   _____ strong
   _____ nothin'

Your next two poems will have an ABCB rhyme scheme. Only the second and fourth lines will rhyme.

5. _____ guy

_____ Bud

_____ him

_____ dud

6. _____ night

_____ red

_____ stairs

_____ dread

Write a rhyming poem on the following lines. You may use whatever rhyme scheme you like. (Feel free to write additional rhyme poems on a separate sheet of paper.)

7. _____

_____

_____

_____

SKILL BUILDING

Pronouns—Subject, Possessive, Object

You've learned that pronouns are words that take the place of nouns. Pronouns can change form. The form of a pronoun depends on its relationship to the other words in the sentence.

For example, a pronoun can be the subject of a sentence.

She writes poetry as a hobby.
Sometimes we read the poems aloud in class.
I enjoy reading poetry.

A pronoun can show possession.

Her poems are usually short.
Our class likes poetry.
My father had a poem printed in a magazine.

A pronoun can be used as the **object** of a verb. That is, *(a)* the pronoun can receive the action of the verb.

The teacher thanked them.

Or *(b)* it can tell to whom or for whom the action of the verb is done.

The poet cooked us a delicious meal.

A pronoun also can be used after words such as *to, at, in, under, from,* and *for.*

Sue Kim likes to have poems read to her.

Circle the correct pronoun in each pair given in parentheses ( ). You may use the chart at the top of page 57 to guide you.

My Land Is Fair for Any Eyes to See

(My/Me) land is fair for any eyes to see—

Now look, (me/my) friends—look to the east and the west—

Hills lined with pine and gum and black-oak tree—

Now to the east (your/you) see the fertile valley!

This land is mine, (I/me) sing of (it/its) to (you/yours)—

(Me/My) land beneath the skies of white and blue.

This land is mine, for (me/I) am part of it.

(I/Me) am the land, for (its/it) is part of me—

(Us/We) are akin and thus (us/our) kinship be!

It would make (I/me) a brother to the tree!

And far as eyes can see this land is (me/mine).

Not for one foot of it (me/I) have a deed—

To own this land (I/me) do not need a deed—

(Them/They) all belong to me—gum, oak, and pine.

By Jesse Stuart

SUBJECT PRONOUNS		PRONOUNS THAT SHOW POSSESSION		OBJECT PRONOUNS	
I	it	my	his	me	it
you	we	mine	its	you	us
he	they	your	our	him	them
she		yours	ours	her	
		her	their		
		hers	theirs		

THINKING ABOUT WRITING

1. Exchange the poems you wrote on pages 54 and 55 with a classmate. Look for similarities and differences in each other's work. Comment on any strong points or weak points in the poems. For example, *(a)* Does each poem have a logical order? *(b)* Are some lines too long or too short? *(c)* Does the last poem have a rhyme scheme?

2. Which of your own poems do you like best? On a separate sheet of paper, write a short paragraph that tells which one of your poems is your favorite. Give reasons for your answer.

3. Can you improve your word order and choice of words? *Make any changes you feel would make your meaning clearer.*

4. In this lesson you wrote poetry. Your writing in the previous six lessons was prose, the usual form of written expression. On your paper, list some of the major differences you notice between poetry and prose.

SKILL BUILDING

5. Look over your poems. Make sure that you have capitalized all proper nouns.

6. In poetry, the first word of each line is usually capitalized. Capitalize these words if you have not already done so.

7. What differences do you see in the way punctuation marks are used in poetry and prose? Discuss these differences on your paper.

8. Examine your handling of pronouns in your poems. Correct any errors you find.

FACTS, FACTS

One complaint that students often make when asked to write is "I don't know how to get started." What's the answer? How *do* you get started writing? One of the most important steps is simply to organize your information beforehand.

We gave lists of historical facts to students in Fort Worth, Texas. The students studied the lists. Then they began organizing the facts. They decided which bits of information had something in common. Finally, they wrote their paragraphs.

Benjamin Franklin was a great man who invented more things than you probably realize. One of his inventions was the harmonica. Another was the street lamp. He even invented bifocal eyeglasses.

Marie Anjou

Something should be done about the horrible loss of animal life. In the last 2,000 years, more than 110 species of animals have become extinct. Seventy percent of these species have died out in just the last century. About 600 other species are presently endangered.

Jaime Torres

The ancient Egyptians were the first to wear wedding rings. Also, they started the custom of wearing the ring on the third finger of the left hand. They did this because they believed that a large vein ran directly from that finger to the heart. The heart, they thought, was the source of love.

Mandy Joers

THINKING ABOUT WHAT YOU HAVE READ

Answer in complete sentences.

1. Which paragraph do you think is the most interesting? Explain your answer.

_____

_____

2. In which paragraph does the writer show anger? Which words show this anger?

_____

_____

3. Marie Anjou's paragraph shows respect for Benjamin Franklin and his accomplishments. How does expressing this feeling affect her writing? Is the paragraph weaker or stronger as a result? Give reasons for your answer.

_____

_____

_____

4. With what kind of sentence do all the writings begin? How many supporting sentences make up the body of each paragraph?

_____

_____

5. Benjamin Franklin really invented more than 20 different things. Marie Anjou wrote about only 3. Would her paragraph have been better if she had mentioned all 20? Support your answer with reasons.

_____

_____

_____

Thinking About Writing

Three-Sentence Paragraphs: Facts and Feelings

Writers often use what is called the *three-sentence paragraph*. Such a paragraph contains a topic sentence backed up by three supporting sentences.

Because such a paragraph is brief, it is important to use only the most interesting and appropriate details.

I.

Each of the following paragraphs begins with a topic sentence followed by *four* supporting sentences. One of these supporting sentences is not appropriate to the paragraph. Find this sentence and cross it out. Then, on a separate sheet of paper, explain why you crossed out the sentence that you did. At the end of the activity, you should have four good three-sentence paragraphs.

1. Some foods got their names in very interesting ways. The sundae takes its name from the fact that its inventor would only serve the dish on Sundays. The sandwich was named after the Earl of Sandwich, an Englishman who liked eating pieces of meat between slices of bread. And the doughnut takes its name from the fact that it was first served to "doughboys," United States soldiers of World War I. The amazing fact about bread is that no one really knows how this all-important food got its name.

2. Throughout history there have been reports of some extremely "strange rains." For example, one day in Romania thousands of black worms came down during a storm. In Butte County, California, a catfish mysteriously fell out of the sky. In Sacramento, California, it once rained thousands of lizards. Last but not least, Padebon, Germany, once suffered a downpour of both water and snails.

3. Behind the names of some famous U.S. political figures there are interesting stories. Benito Mussolini, for example, was named after Benito Juárez, a former president of Mexico. George Washington, who led the colonies in their battle for independence from England, was named after King George II of England. Harry S Truman, the 33d U.S. president, had a letter for his middle name; the *S* is not an abbreviation, it's a name. Ulysses S. Grant, the 18th U.S. president, accidentally got a new name due to a mix-up in his records while he was attending West Point; his real name was Hiram Ulysses Grant, not Ulysses S. Grant.

4. There have been many unusual trials down through history. For example, there was the case of the giraffe that was sued for not making its refrigerator payments. And there was the man who was charged with shoplifting one grape. There have even been trials that lasted half a dozen years. But the strangest case on record may be the one in which a woman filed a $100,000 damage suit against God for letting a lightning bolt strike her home.

Adding your feeling or opinion to a paragraph lets your reader know where you stand on your subject. Feelings and opinions can also add life to your writing. Compare, for example, the following two topic sentences.

Lions are terrifying but interesting animals.
I am going to tell you about lions.

The writer of the first sentence seems interested in the subject and eager to tell the reader about it. The second sentence is lifeless and dull.

II.

Circle the letter of the topic sentence in each of the following pairs that is livelier and gives a clearer picture of the writer's feelings.

1. **a.** Here are some facts about the lizard.
    b. Lizards are strange, feisty characters.

2. **a.** What you don't know about food additives may just kill you!
    b. There are a great many additives in your food.

3. **a.** It is hard to think of a finer human being than Father Damien.
    b. Much is known about the life of Father Damien.

4. **a.** John Paul Jones was not the superman everybody has long thought him to be.
    b. I will now tell you about John Paul Jones.

5. **a.** Boxing is a very bad sport.
    b. Busted heads and broken dreams, that's what boxing is about!

III.

Rewrite each topic sentence that follows in a way that gives it life and feeling.

1. Thomas Edison was an inventor.

    _____

2. There is a lot to be learned about tigers.

    _____

3. Football is the subject I am going to write about.

    _____

4. Helen Keller did many things during her life.

    _____

Getting Ready to Write

Soon you are going to write a paragraph in which you give information about some aspect of sports. The following activities will give you the facts you need. They will also help you to organize your paragraph. These are, you remember, the two key steps in getting started on a piece of writing.

I.

Read the following list of sports facts carefully before going on.

1. The first golf balls were made of boiled feathers stuffed into a hard leather pouch.
2. Dwight Eisenhower, the 34th U.S. president, was a running back for West Point.
3. "Babe" Ruth's first name was not Babe; it was George.
4. The first Ping-Pong balls were made of tightly wound string.
5. William Wrigley, Jr., the chewing-gum manufacturer, started the Chicago Cubs.
6. In the early days of professional football, the penalty for clipping was 25 yards.
7. In the early days of basketball, three penalties counted as a point scored for the other team.
8. Queen Elizabeth I of England was a skilled hunter.
9. In basketball, each team originally had seven players.
10. Richard Nixon, 37th president of the United States, played tackle for Whittier College.
11. In the early days of baseball, it took four strikes to make an out, not three.
12. The first Ping-Pong table was an ordinary living-room table.
13. The first Ping-Pong net consisted of books set end down on the middle of the table.

14. A touchdown in football was originally worth four points, not six as it is today.

15. Gerald Ford, 38th president of the U.S., was a center for the University of Michigan football team.

16. Early billiard balls were made of brass.

17. In the early days of baseball, a fly ball caught on one bounce was an out.

18. The first basketball backboards were made of wire mesh.

19. The Green Bay Packers football team was started in 1921 by J. E. Clair of the Acme Packing Company, Green Bay, Wisconsin.

20. In early baseball, the batter ran clockwise around the diamond; first base was where third is today.

II.

Now it's time to organize the information you just read. As you complete each item that follows, you will see connections among many of the facts in Part I.

1. a. On the line, write the numbers of the facts about early sports equipment. Two numbers have been written for you. _1, 4_____

    b. Now be more specific. List only the numbers of the facts about the original Ping-Pong equipment. _____

2. a. On the line, write the numbers of the facts about famous people and sports.

    _____

    b. Again, be more specific. List only the numbers of the facts about U.S. presidents who played football. _____

3. a. On the line, write the numbers of the facts about the rules and types of plays in early sports.

    _____

    b. Narrow down your list once more. Write only the numbers of the facts about the rules and plays in early baseball. _____

III.

Your answers to items 1b, 2b, and 3b in Part II give you the facts you need for a three-sentence paragraph. After you complete the two steps that follow, you will be ready to write the paragraph.

1. Put a check (√) in front of the topic you will write about.

    _____ Early Ping-Pong equipment (Part II, 1b)

    _____ United States presidents who played football (Part II, 2b)

    _____ Rules and types of plays in early baseball (Part II, 3b)

2. On the lines, write a topic sentence for your paragraph.

    _____

    _____

Writing the Three-Sentence Paragraph

On a separate sheet of paper, write a three-sentence paragraph about early Ping-Pong equipment, U.S. presidents who played football, or the rules and the types of plays in early baseball. Remember that a three-sentence paragraph is made up of a topic sentence and three supporting sentences. Remember also that your feelings and opinions will help add life to your topic sentence. Use your answers to "Getting Ready to Write" (pages 62 through 64) to guide you.

SKILL BUILDING

Commas

The comma is the most often used punctuation mark in English. It occurs even more frequently than the period, which ends roughly 90 percent of all sentences. The **comma (,)** is used to divide the parts of a sentence. It marks pauses in thought.

Learning to handle the comma takes a good deal of time and study. There are many rules that govern its use. As you go on through this book, you will learn a number of these rules. But let's leave the rules alone for now. Instead, we'll start by getting a feel for the way this mark is used.

Each of the following sentences is broken into its parts. The breaks come at the points where commas are placed. First, number the sentence parts in the correct order. Then write the sentence on a sheet of paper, as you see in the example. Remember to add capital letters and periods where they are needed.

EXAMPLE: __2__ then at war with the United States,

__1__ it was discovered in 1942 that Adolf Hitler,

__3__ owned over 8,000 acres of valuable land in Colorado

It was discovered in 1942 that Adolf Hitler, then at war with the United States, owned over 8,000 acres of valuable land in Colorado.

1. _____ $184 billion on housing,

_____ and $95 billion on clothing

_____ U.S. citizens spend $261 billion a year on food,

2. _____ even by accident,

_____ was death

_____ the ancient Egyptian punishment for killing a cat,

3. _____ and "talking" movies were just science-fiction fantasies

_____ until quite recently,

_____ sliding doors,

_____ such things as electric stoves,

4. _____ flannel shirts,

_____ in contrast to the baseball uniforms worn today,

_____ and woolen pants

_____ the early uniforms consisted of straw hats,

5. _____ a dishwasher 11 years,

_____ on the average,

_____ and a television 12 years

_____ a refrigerator can be expected to last 15 years,

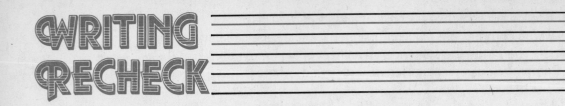

THINKING ABOUT WRITING

1. Study the three-sentence paragraph you wrote on your paper. Does it begin with a strong topic sentence that tells what the whole paragraph is about? Is the body of the paragraph made up of three sentences that give facts supporting the topic sentence? If the answer to either question is no, make the necessary changes in your paragraph.

2. Did you put life and feeling into your paragraph? Did you communicate your feelings or opinions about your subject? If not, write a new paragraph. Pay special attention to the wording of your topic sentence.

3. Take a second look at the topic sentences of the four exercise paragraphs on page 60. Underline those words that communicate a feeling about the subject.

SKILL BUILDING

4. Exchange papers with a classmate. Check her or his paragraph for the following items:

   _____ capitalization errors

   _____ incorrect or missing end-of-sentence punctuation

   _____ run-on sentences

   _____ fragments

   _____ incorrect use of pronouns

   Correct any errors that your classmate finds in your paragraph.

5. Think about the use of commas in your paragraph. Are there any places without commas where you think commas might belong? If so, consult your teacher.

THE FRIENDLY LETTER

Imagine that your Uncle Mortimer has written to invite you to spend the summer on his farm in Tennessee. You may or may not want to go. Regardless, you have to write a letter to your uncle either accepting or rejecting his offer.

This is the situation we presented to over 50 students in Los Angeles, California. They had to write an answer in friendly-letter form to this fictional uncle. What they would say was left entirely to their imagination. Below are a few of the students' letters. As you will see, the answers varied greatly.

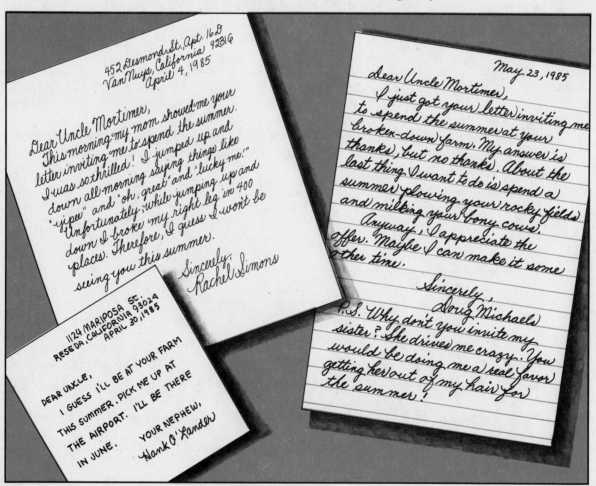

452 Desmond St., Apt. 16D
Van Nuys, California 92316
April 4, 1985

Dear Uncle Mortimer,
This morning my mom showed me your letter inviting me to spend the summer. I was so thrilled! I jumped up and down all morning saying things like "yipee" and "oh, great" and "lucky me!" Unfortunately, while jumping up and down I broke my right leg in 400 places. Therefore, I guess I won't be seeing you this summer.

Sincerely,
Rachel Simons

1124 MARIPOSA ST.
RESEDA, CALIFORNIA 93024
APRIL 30, 1985

DEAR UNCLE,
I GUESS I'LL BE AT YOUR FARM THIS SUMMER. PICK ME UP AT THE AIRPORT. I'LL BE THERE IN JUNE.

YOUR NEPHEW,
Hank O'Lander

May 23, 1985

Dear Uncle Mortimer,
I just got your letter inviting me to spend the summer at your broken-down farm. My answer is thanks, but no thanks. About the last thing I want to do is spend a summer plowing your rocky fields and milking your bony cows.
Anyway, I appreciate the offer. Maybe I can make it some other time.

Sincerely,
Doug Michaels
P.S. Why don't you invite my sister? She drives me crazy. You would be doing me a real favor getting her out of my hair for the summer!

67

THINKING ABOUT WHAT YOU HAVE READ

Answer in complete sentences.

1. Is Rachel Simons's letter a serious one? What is she really saying in her letter? Explain your answer.

_____

_____

_____

2. The friendly letter follows a standard form. Compare the extremely rude letter by Doug Michaels with the other letters. What part of the friendly-letter form is missing from his letter?

_____

_____

3. The form of Hank O'Lander's letter is correct and complete. The body of the letter, however, lacks important details. What information should Hank have included?

_____

_____

_____

4. All the letters are written to an imaginary person. Which letter is most like one you would actually write in the situation given? Which letter would you be least likely to send to a real person? Be ready to discuss your answers.

_____

_____

_____

_____

5. The letter by Doug Michaels ends with a *P.S.* The *P.S.* is an abbreviation of *postscript.* Look up the word *postscript* in a dictionary. Write its definition below.

_____

_____

_____

THINKING ABOUT WRITING

The Friendly Letter—Form and Tone

Imagine finding this unsigned "letter" in your mailbox.

We've changed the time and place for the party. See you there!

The letter would leave you with a head full of question marks: What party? When? Where? Last but not least, you'd want to know who wrote the letter.

Now imagine that a few weeks later you find out the letter was written by your ex-good-friend Mickey Mouthskid. Furious, you pen the following letter.

Heading <
912 Mooreland St., Apt. 31
Dayton, OH 85243

November 18, 1985

Dear Mickey, > **Salutation**

I am writing to tell you and *show* you how to write a letter.

First, before you start your letter, write your address near the top right-hand corner of the paper. Below that you write the date (if you know it!). Carefully put a comma between the city and state. Then stick another one between the day and the year. Your address and the date make up the **heading** of the letter.

Start your letter with a **salutation.** The salutation is a greeting to your reader. Even if you don't like the person, you write *Dear* followed by the name of the person to whom you're writing. Sometimes you will use a title, such as *Mr., Ms.,* or *Mrs.,* and then the person's last name: *Dear Mr. Rogers.* Remember to capitalize all the words in the salutation and to put periods after abbreviations. And stick a comma after the salutation.

Next comes the **body** of your letter. It is the actual message you are sending. It is everything I have written after the salutation of the letter that you're reading right now.

You end a letter with a **closing.** It is a way of saying "goodbye" or "it's all over" or *"adios"* to your reader. *Yours truly* and *Sincerely yours* are two closings that are often used. Capitalize only the first word in the closing. Put a comma, then sign your idiotic name.

Believe me, I am not writing this because I want an apology. I just think it's about time you learned how to write a letter.

Body

Closing < Your former friend,

Signature < *Ima Notforgivingyou*

69

I.

The following letter contains a number of errors. Rewrite it on a separate sheet of paper, correcting every error you find.

331 Dakota St
Milwaukee, WI 47281

Mr. Tate

Thanks a million for your strange gift. Getting a whole box of live rattlesnakes was something I didn't expect!

I'm sorry to say that my mother and brother have already been bitten three times each, but they are both okay, and the doctor expects them to live.

P.S. In the note you sent along, you didn't tell me the names of the rattlesnakes. Please write and tell me their names.

yours Truly mike

II.

Below is the outline of an envelope. Imagine you are sending a letter to Dr. and Mrs. Frankenstein. They live at 1234 Vampire Blvd., Treeless, California. The zip code is 90010. In the large shaded area, address the envelope to the Frankensteins. In the upper left-hand corner, write your name and return address.

Tone is a writer's attitude toward his or her subject or reader. For example, a writer may show sorrow or anger or joy—or any other emotion—in a piece of writing.

III.

Put yourself in the place of a 15-year-old who is celebrating a birthday. Aunt Mildred has sent you a gift: a size-two gray blanket sleeper with bunny pictures on it. You sit down to write Aunt Mildred a thank-you note. The job turns out to be much tougher than you expected. Soon your desk is covered with different draft letters as you struggle to get just the right tone.

Match each thank-you note that follows with the word at the right that best describes the tone. Write the letter of the tone in the blank before the thank-you note.

_____ 1. I thought you truly knew me and cared about me and remembered me. But you sent me a blanket sleeper for a little kid! I guess you *don't* know me or care about me at all.

    A. confused

_____ 2. I'm not sure, but was there some mistake about the gift you sent me? I received a size-two blanket sleeper, but I wear a size 49, extra large. I don't understand.

    B. polite

    C. hurt

_____ 3. Thanks very much for your gift. It's been a while since we've seen each other, and I really appreciate your thinking of me.

Getting Ready to Write

The following activity will help you get ready to write a friendly letter inviting someone to a party. The person to whom you write may be either real or imaginary. You will make up the details about the party.

Answer in complete sentences.

1. Who are you inviting to the party?

   _____

2. What kind of party will it be?

   _____

3. Where will the party be? Give both the name of the place and the address.

   _____

4. What is the date of the party? At what time will it start, and when will it end?

   _____

5. Give any other information that the person receiving the letter needs to know.

   _____

Writing a Friendly Letter

On a separate sheet of paper, write a friendly letter inviting someone to an imaginary party. Be sure to include all the necessary details. Use your answers to "Getting Ready to Write" (above) to help you. Also be sure to use the correct form for a friendly letter. Follow the example of friendly-letter form on page 69.

SKILL BUILDING

Commas

You've written commas in sentences many times. And, like most writers, you probably wondered and worried if you were putting them in the right places.

You won't have to wonder or worry when you tackle the sentences in the activity that follows. Each sentence tells you where the commas go and why they go there. Just do what the sentences tell you. At the same time you'll be learning some of the rules for placing commas, which you can use in writing sentences of your own.

Add commas to the following sentences according to the directions given in the sentences.

EXAMPLE: This sentence has two independent clauses, and that's why you need a comma before the conjunction.

1. A banana an apricot and a grapefruit make up a series of items that requires a comma after the second and fourth words in this sentence.

2. You are being spoken to Bob so put a comma before and after your name.

3. Bob you should put one comma after your name (because you're still being spoken to).

4. Because this sentence begins with a subordinate clause followed by a main clause you need to put a comma after the 13th word in this sentence.

5. Run to the store buy a loaf of bread and place a comma after the fourth and ninth words in the series of actions that makes up the sentence you're now reading.

6. This sentence consists of two independent clauses joined by a conjunction so you have to put a comma before the conjunction.

7. Furthermore this sentence needs a comma after the first word (because it serves as an introduction to the rest of the sentence).

8. Mrs. Douglas my English teacher says that apposition makes it necessary for you to put commas after the second and fifth words above.

9. The tall dark-haired man said you must put a comma between the two adjectives describing him (between the second and third words in this sentence).

10. Put a comma here another one here and then check to make sure there is a period at the end of the sentence.

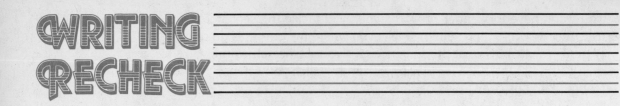

WRITING RECHECK

THINKING ABOUT WRITING

1. Look over the format of your friendly letter. Check (√) that you have included each of the following parts and that each is correct in every detail.

    _____ heading

    _____ salutation

    _____ body

    _____ closing

    _____ signature

2. Give your letter to a classmate. Have him or her check (√) to see that all of the information in the following list is given.

    _____ what kind of party it is going to be

    _____ where the party will be

    _____ the date and time of the party

    If any of these details are missing from your letter, add them in a postscript (P.S.).

3. What is the tone of your letter? Describe it on a separate sheet of paper.

SKILL BUILDING

4. The Skill Building activity on page 73 gives a brief overview of some of the rules for using commas. See if you can apply one or more of these rules to your letter. That is, add commas where the rules indicate they are necessary.

5. Check your letter for capitalization errors, incorrect end-of-sentence punctuation, run-on sentences, sentence fragments, and incorrect pronoun forms. Correct any errors you find.

10 WAKE-UP STORIES

In this lesson there are going to be some eye-opening changes in your life. They'll be make-believe, and they'll be temporary. Yet the changes will occur, nonetheless.

Start by reading the story "Who's Who?" It will give you an idea of what you are letting yourself in for.

Who's Who?

It still seems impossible. I don't know how it happened. And I don't really know *why* it happened. I guess everything somehow started with my conversation last Tuesday with Traci, my best friend.

Traci said, "Janet, I wish I were more like you. You get good grades, you're good at sports, and your parents never hassle you."

I answered that I wished I were her. I said she had a better figure, beautiful hair, and a boyfriend who was really good to her.

That was just the first part of our conversation. We went on and on for a long time. I thought it would be great being Traci. She thought it would be great being me.

That night I went to sleep thinking about what we had said. Maybe that is what caused it. I just don't know. Anyway, when I woke up I felt very different and very strange. I looked around my room, but it wasn't mine! It was Traci's room!

I got out of bed. I went to the mirror. I couldn't believe what I saw. I had turned into Traci!

Traci's mom came into the room. She told me she had to leave early for work, and she had left lunch money on the kitchen table. I was still in a state of shock. I didn't know what to say to her. I just mumbled, in Traci's voice, "Okay. Thanks."

For a long time I just sat there in the room. I didn't know what to do. Then I had an idea. I would go to school. The real Traci would be there! I could talk to her and perhaps figure out what had happened.

I put on Traci's clothes, took Traci's books and Traci's lunch money, and headed for school.

I arrived just before my first-period class was to begin. It was U.S. history. Traci and I had the class together.

I walked into the room. I looked at Traci's seat, but it was empty. Then I looked at my seat. Sitting in it was me! No, it was Traci; but she had turned into me!

With a frightened expression on her face, she walked to where I was standing in the doorway. Then we talked in the hall.

"I'm you, and you're me!" she said.

"I know," I said. "And what are we going to do?"

"We can't tell anybody. They'll just think we're joking or that we're nuts. I guess we'll just have to go on being each other."

And that's what we decided to do. I'm Traci, and Traci is me. It's been that way for several days now, and I don't like it. I found out that I don't like Traci's boyfriend, and I don't like getting Traci's bad grades. I miss sports, and I miss my family and my home. Besides, it's just too weird being somebody else. I only wish I were me again.

THINKING ABOUT WHAT YOU HAVE READ

Answer in complete sentences.

1. On page 20 you were told that the plot of a story is its framework. It is the most important events that happen. What is the plot of "Who's Who?"? Below, briefly describe the plot by telling the main events in the order in which they happened.

   _____

   _____

   _____

   _____

   _____

   _____

2. Do you like the story? Explain your answer.

   _____

   _____

   _____

3. "Who's Who?" is told by one of the characters in the story. Who is that character?

   _____

4. The *theme* of a story is the message or the idea behind it. It is the point the author is trying to make. What is the theme of "Who's Who?"? Does it have something to do with "being yourself"? Explain your answer.

   _____

   _____

   _____

5. Have you ever wanted to be (or to be like) someone else? If not, explain why. If so, explain who the person was and why you wanted to be (or to be like) that person.

   _____

   _____

   _____

THINKING ABOUT WRITING

Point of View

Every story, whether written or spoken, has a teller. Another word for *story-teller* is *narrator*. The term **point of view** is used to describe the narrator's position in relation to the story.

At the most basic level, there are two points of view from which a story can be told. These two points of view are called *first person* and *third person*.

First person: The narrator is inside the story and is one of the characters. The narrator refers to himself or herself throughout, using such pronouns as *I, me, my, mine,* and *myself.* The story "Who's Who?" is written from the first-person point of view.

Third person: The narrator is outside the story and is not one of the characters. The narrator never refers to herself or himself directly but instead reports the thoughts and the actions of others.

The following story is written from the third-person point of view. Change the point of view to first person by changing nouns and pronouns. The first three changes have been made for you.

The Fur-bearing Stranger

When ~~Joey Marsupial~~ *I* woke up, ~~he~~ *I* knew right away that something was wrong. ~~His~~ *My* arms had gotten very short, and they were furry! And his feet were sticking out of the bottom of the covers. They were huge feet, and they weren't even his! They were some sort of animal's feet!

Joey hopped out of bed and over to the mirror. He almost fainted. He had turned into a kangaroo!

From the kitchen came the voices of his mother and father. He hopped down the hall. Then he bounded into the kitchen. His mother looked up and dropped a plate of scrambled eggs. His father stared in disbelief.

"I turned into a kangaroo!" Joey tried to say. But it came out as "Skroink adolo urk skroink!"

Joey's mom tossed a handful of hash-browns at him. His dad rolled up a newspaper and started hitting him over the head. They, of course, had no way of knowing that this fur-bearing stranger was their son!

"Don't, Pops!" Joey tried to say. This came out as "Eeko, Gopboi!"

His dad kept hitting him, and his mom was screaming like crazy. Joey had no choice. He hopped out the back door, hightailing it down the street.

There was an interesting story on the news the other day. It probably had something to do with Joey. According to the story, a kangaroo was spotted down by the docks trying to buy a ticket for the next ship to Australia.

Getting Ready to Write

Follow the directions for items 1 and 2. As you do, you'll be getting ready to write a story in which you wake up one day as someone or something else.

1. It is an ordinary morning. You wake up in bed to find that you have changed while asleep into somebody or something else. The following list includes some of the forms in which you might wake up. After studying the list carefully, circle the "change" you think would make the most interesting story. You may add an item of your choice on the line.

   robot   bear   deer   your brother or sister   bee   snake   elephant

   one of your teachers   person from the past   _____

2. The plot of a story is its framework. It is the outline of the most important events. Below, plot your story. List the most important things that will happen in the order in which they'll occur.

   _____

   _____

   _____

   _____

Writing a Wake-up Story

On a separate sheet of paper, write a short story in which you wake up as the person, animal, or thing you chose in item 1 of "Getting Ready to Write." Use the plot outline you wrote in item 2 as a guide while you work on your story.

SKILL BUILDING

Commas in a Series

Nouns, you remember, are words that name persons, places, and things. In some sentences, you will find several nouns grouped together in a *series,* or list. Notice how commas are used in the following underlined series of nouns.

<u>Dean Martin</u>, <u>Al Pacino</u>, and <u>Frank Sinatra</u> are all well-known actors.

My sister collects odd facts about <u>movies</u>, <u>records</u>, and <u>books</u>.

Some sentences contain a list of *verbs,* or words that name actions. Commas are used to separate actions just as they are used to separate the names of people, places, and things in sentences.

Anita <u>read</u> the book, <u>found</u> an interesting fact, and <u>wrote</u> it in her notebook.

I.

Each sentence that follows contains a series of nouns. Add commas where they belong. The number in parentheses ( ) after each sentence tells how many commas are needed.

1. Did you know that Winston Churchill Sarah Bernhardt and Benito Mussolini wrote one novel apiece? (2)

2. *Dune M*A*S*H Dubliners* and *Kon-Tiki* were best-selling books that were rejected by 10 or more publishers. (3)

3. The following famous writers all wrote standing up: Lewis Carroll Ernest Hemingway Thomas Jefferson William Saroyan and Virginia Woolf. (4)

4. Thermos zipper escalator cellophane and aspirin are all brand names that became common words. (4)

5. The following words were all common in seventeenth-century English but are largely forgotten today: *fellowfeel aimcrier keak lip-clap murfles snirtle* and *wurp.* (6)

6. Chang Martin Schultz Smith and Garcia are five of the most common last names in the world. (4)

7. *Celsius pompadour boycott diesel* and *lynch* are common words that began as people's last names. (4)

8. The following languages are the most widely spoken on Earth: Chinese English Russian Spanish Hindi and Arabic. (5)

II.

Each sentence that follows contains a series of actions that should be separated by commas. Add commas where they belong. The number in parentheses ( ) after each sentence tells how many commas should be added.

EXAMPLE: In 1933 a kitten fell out of an airplane landed on the ground and walked away.

In 1933 a kitten fell out of an airplane, landed on the ground, and walked away.

1. In 1977 Harvey Gatly stepped into a boxing ring took a mighty swing and knocked himself out. (2)

2. In 1940 a German pilot spotted a ship dropped several bombs watched the ship sink and later learned that the ship belonged to Germany. (3)

3. In 1978 the people of Coacaloco chased the mayor captured him forced him to eat 12 pounds of bananas then demanded his resignation. (3)

4. In 1972 a skydiver named Bob Hail jumped from a plane discovered that his parachute wouldn't open fell 3,300 feet (1,006 meters) landed on his face and then walked away with only a broken nose. (4)

THINKING ABOUT WRITING

1. Is your "wake-up" story written from the first-person point of view? If it isn't, go back and rewrite your story, using the first-person point of view.

2. Is the tone of your story humorous or serious? On your paper, describe the tone of your story.

SKILL BUILDING

3. In the Skill Building activities on pages 80–81 you added commas in a series of nouns and a series of actions. Look over your story. Are there any places where you listed several nouns or actions but did not separate them with commas? If so, add the commas now.

4. Check your story for the following problems: capitalization errors, incorrect end-of-sentence punctuation, run-on sentences, sentence fragments, and incorrect use of pronouns. Correct any errors you find.

MAKE-BELIEVE "BIOGRAPHY"

The word *biography* comes to us from the Greeks. *Bios,* in Greek, means "life." *Graphein* means "to write." Thus, a biography is the written story of a person's life.

A biography is always factual. But Marta Rubens of Indianapolis, Indiana, wrote a funny one that she made up herself. Marta wrote the life story of an imaginary person she called Holden Breathburger.

The Amazing Balloon Boy

Holden Breathburger was born in 1909 on a farm in Blowout, Indiana. His father was 104 at the time of his birth, and his mother was 98. They had no idea that their newborn son would turn out to be very weird.

At first Holden seemed normal. He was just a typical, fat little baby. He drooled a lot, threw food at his parents, and drew pictures on the wall with his crayons. His mother and father thought he was a great kid.

Then one day when Holden was five years old something strange happened. He took a big deep breath and inflated like a balloon. Slowly he rose off the ground and started floating around the room! His parents ran after him, yelling for him to come down. After about an hour or so, Holden got tired of holding his breath. He exhaled and drifted down to the floor.

Holden's parents begged him not to turn himself into a human blimp ever again. Holden promised he wouldn't. And he kept his promise until he was 12. Then one day at school, a bully by the name of Les Fiteman threatened to beat up Holden. Holden puffed himself up and floated away. Les Fiteman started crying. Kids screamed and pointed. Teachers fainted.

The principal called Mr. and Mrs. Breathburger. He said he was kicking Holden out of school for scaring everyone. Heartbroken, Holden ran away and joined the circus. He worked there for 15 years as the Amazing Balloon Boy.

Holden finally got tired of the circus. He decided he wanted to do something great and important. He traveled to the East Coast. When he got there, he announced that he was going to do something no one had done before. He was going to be the first person to fly across the Atlantic—without an airplane!

Ma and Pa Breathburger stood on the docks with hundreds of other on-lookers. They watched as Holden inflated himself and sailed out across the ocean, waving bye-bye.

Holden was never seen or heard from again.

THINKING ABOUT WHAT YOU HAVE READ

Answer in complete sentences.

1. If you were a teacher, what grade would you give the story by Marta Rubens? Explain your reasons for the grade you would give.

_____

_____

_____

2. Marta's story is *fictional,* or made-up. Below, give three details from the story that show it is fictional.

_____

_____

_____

_____

_____

3. What do you think of the ending of the "biography"? Is it a good ending, in your opinion?

_____

_____

_____

4. From what point of view is Holden's life story told, first person or third person? Support your answer by pointing out at least one specific detail from the story.

_____

_____

_____

5. How would you describe Marta's tone? For example, is it lighthearted, serious, sarcastic? Refer to specific sentences in the "biography" when explaining your answer.

_____

_____

_____

Thinking About Writing

Paragraphing

Almost any kind of extended writing should be broken into paragraphs. Most paragraphs consist of several sentences. All the sentences develop the same main idea. This main idea is stated in the topic sentence.

A biography is an example of an extended written composition. It needs to be divided into paragraphs. Where should the paragraph divisions occur? Keep in mind that a biography is often written in *chronological order*. That is, events are written in the order in which they happened. Thus, the first paragraph of a biography usually gives facts about the person's birth—when and where. The other paragraphs describe events at later stages in the person's life. The final paragraph brings the life story to a close, perhaps by telling what the person is doing today.

Read carefully the following "biography" of an imaginary person. Then, in the blanks, number the paragraphs in chronological order.

The Predicaments of Patience Plodder

_____ At the age of 40, Patience decided it was time to get a job. She phoned the president of the United States and asked about job opportunities. The president was thrilled to hear from Patience and immediately put her in touch with people at the Pentagon.

_____ Even as a child, Patience clearly was going to turn out like her parents. Everyday the three of them just sat around and watched TV. They always watched the same station, even if they didn't like the program. Changing stations was just too tiring for them.

_____ That was the end of Patience's school career. She spent the next four years in bed at home, trying to recover from the ordeal. On good days she would watch the grass grow.

_____ Patience Plodder was born at home in 1992. She was born at home because her mom, Petunia Plodder, was unable to walk to the hospital. And her father, Pete Plodder, was too tired to drive her there. The hospital was across the street.

_____ Today Patience is a fighter pilot. She is a changed person and has shed her lazy ways. If they had the energy, her parents would be proud of her.

_____ When Patience turned 15, her mom and dad decided it was time for her to go to school. On her first day in school, Patience was told to erase the chalkboard. She did her best, but the eraser was just too heavy. Poor Patience fell to the floor, exhausted and gasping for breath. She was carried to the nurse's office. There she slept on a cot for eight weeks, until her parents got up enough energy to come and get her.

Getting Ready to Write

Soon you will write a "biography" of an imaginary person. The following activity will help you get ready to write.

Each box that follows stands for one of the paragraphs in the "biography" you will write. In each box, give the information asked for. (Your answers may be serious or funny, depending on the kind of "biography" you want to write.)

1. Think of a name for the imaginary person whose "life story" you are going to write. Then write where and when this person was born. Finally, give the names of the person's parents.

2. Describe what this person was like as a baby. Was there anything special about him or her?

3. What are some of the things the person did as a teenager? Jot them down.

4. Jot down what the person did as an adult.

5. What is the person doing today? Write your answer in the box.

Writing a "Biography"

On a separate sheet of paper, write the life story of an imaginary person. Use the notes you made in "Getting Ready to Write" on pages 86–87 to guide you. Think of each box you filled in as a separate paragraph. Be sure to indent the first line of each paragraph, as you see in the following line in this book.

Feel free to include information in addition to what you noted in the boxes on pages 86–87. Just remember to paragraph the added information correctly. (If you need help in paragraphing, go back and reread "Thinking about Writing" on page 85.) Remember, too, that you're telling the whole story in chronological order.

SKILL BUILDING

Commas and Appositives

An **appositive** is a noun, or a substitute for a noun, which is placed beside another noun to explain it more fully.

NOUN	APPOSITIVE	
Lorne Green,	the actor,	was born in Canada.

NOUN	APPOSITIVE	
Canada,	a North American country,	was once Lorne Green's home.

In the first example sentence, the term the actor is an appositive. Set off with commas, it explains who Lorne Green is. In the second example, the appositive a North American country—also set off with commas—explains what Canada is.

I.

Add commas to set off the appositives in the following sentences. Each sentence contains one appositive. The number at the end of each sentence tells you how many commas you need to add.

1. Albert Einstein the famous scientist was once asked to become president of Israel. (2)

2. Pancho Villa the Mexican revolutionary once appeared in a U.S. motion picture. (2)

3. The derby a type of hat was named after an annual horse race in England. (2)

4. Shrapnel the pieces of metal found in artillery shells was invented by a man named Henry Shrapnel. (2)

5. Teddy bears are named for Teddy Roosevelt the 26th U.S. president. (1)

6. The gardenia a type of flower was named after Alexander Garden a scientist from Scotland. (3)

II.

Each sentence that follows has a blank following a noun. In the blank, add information that helps to explain or identify the noun. The information you add must make sense within the complete sentence.

EXAMPLE: Brooke Shields, _the famous young actress and model_, loves Japanese food.

1. Ronald Reagan, _____, was once a Democrat.

2. Kareem Abdul-Jabbar, _____, likes to play the conga drums in his spare time.

3. Lucille Ball, _____, flunked out of acting school when she was a teenager.

4. Howard Cosell, _____, started talking at the age of nine months.

5. Sean Connery, _____, has the words "Scotland Forever" tattooed on his forearm.

THINKING ABOUT WRITING

1. Look over the "biography" you wrote. Is it broken into paragraphs? If not, go back and mark paragraph divisions now. Also mark any places where you forgot to indent when starting a new paragraph.

2. In the "biography," did you repeat words or information unnecessarily? Did you restate ideas already made clear earlier? If so, remove or rewrite sentences that contain repetitions.

3. Check to be sure that the events in the "biography" you've written are told in chronological order. The story should begin with the imaginary person's birth and progress step by step through his or her adulthood. If the events are not told in chronological order, rewrite your story on a separate sheet of paper.

SKILL BUILDING

4. Study the "biography" of Holden Breathburger on pages 82–83. Find one sentence that contains a series of actions separated by commas. Write it on the following lines.

    _____

    _____

5. In the "biography" of Patience Plodder (page 85), find two sentences that contain appositives. Copy these two sentences on the following lines. Then underline each appositive.

    _____

    _____

    _____

    _____

6. Check your writing for the following problems: capitalization errors, incorrect end-of-sentence punctuation, run-on sentences, fragments, and incorrect pronouns. Correct any errors you find as you go through your writing.

12 CLASS CWRITING

What are your classes like this term? Which are fun? Which are challenging? Are you learning more in some classes than others? Who is your favorite teacher?

Lynda Ryder of Concord, New Hampshire, wrote a composition in which she described her classes. She discussed the classes she liked and those she disliked. She described her teachers. She explained what she did and what she learned from the beginning of her school day to the end.

My Classes

This is my first year at Greenfield. I have five classes. I like three of them. Two of them are—well, not my favorites.

My first-period class is physical education. It is not one of my favorite classes. For one thing, I'm too tired at 8:00 A.M. to be interested in volleyball, soccer, or basketball. Worse, I just hate having PE before all my other classes. I get all sweaty. Even after taking a shower, I feel sticky for the rest of the day.

My second-period class is math, with Mr. Roth. Mr. Roth is okay, but math is a subject I just can't take. I think it's a total drag. The only thing I think about in math is the time when it will be over.

Everything gets better after second period. For third period I have home economics. It's a fun class, and I think the teacher, Mrs. Gomez, is really a super person. If I have a problem, I can always go to Mrs. Gomez, and she will take time to help me. She truly understands people my age.

Fourth period is geography. I don't like the teacher a lot, but I have learned a lot in the class. The teacher, Mr. Waltney, is too strict, but does he ever know how to teach! I think I have learned more from Mr. Waltney than from any other teacher I have ever had.

Period five is English. My teacher is Ms. Elner. She is very young and seems sort of nervous most of the time. She is a very good teacher, so I don't know why she is so nervous. She makes the class interesting and fun.

These are the classes I have this term. All in all, they are pretty good. I think I am getting a good education. I know I am learning a lot.

THINKING ABOUT WHAT YOU HAVE READ

Answer in complete sentences.

1. Why doesn't Lynda like physical education? What specific reasons does she give?

_____

_____

2. According to Lynda, which teacher is most understanding and aware of how teenagers feel? How might this teacher be helpful to Lynda?

_____

_____

3. Lynda thinks Mr. Waltney is too strict, and she doesn't care for him very much. Still, she thinks he is a very good teacher. Have you ever had a teacher like this? Have you ever had a teacher you didn't care for but who taught you well? Explain your answer.

_____

_____

4. Lynda says that her English teacher, Ms. Elner, seems nervous most of the time. Why might a teacher be nervous in class? Give at least three reasons for your answer.

_____

_____

_____

5. What might Lynda do to help Ms. Elner overcome her nervousness?

_____

_____

Thinking About Writing

Paragraphing in Compositions

In Lesson 8, you studied the three-sentence paragraph. You learned that it has a topic sentence and several supporting sentences. The topic sentence states the main idea. The other sentences give information about the main idea.

Have you ever read something in which all the ideas—all the sentences and paragraphs—ran together? If you have, did you find yourself wondering where one paragraph ended and another began? Most of us have read such selections. And for most of us, they were hard to follow.

Like the sentences in a paragraph, the paragraphs in a composition build upon a main thought. They help the reader follow the writer's thinking, step by step. When paragraphs are run together, the reader may not be able to see where the writer is headed in the composition.

Read the following composition carefully. Then, by drawing boxes, set off each paragraph. The first, or introductory, paragraph has been set off for you. You should have a total of nine paragraphs when you've finished the activity.

A Day in My Life

I now go to Whitman High. (I transferred here at midsemester when my parents moved from Phoenix.) I have six classes, not including homeroom. All my classes and teachers are as different from each other as night and day. First I have homeroom. It's pretty simple. The teacher takes attendance and reads the bulletin. Once the teacher is through, I usually spend the rest of the period trying to catch up on my studies. Period one is an art class. The students are awful. There's one group that spends the whole period just painting nonsense. For second period I have English, with Mr. Inan. Mr. Inan is very strict. He also has a strong accent, and sometimes I have trouble understanding what he's saying. I think it's unusual that somebody who doesn't speak English the way we do is teaching us English. My third-period class is history. The teacher is Ms. Van de Waar. She's a great person and a great teacher. She teaches us all sorts of interesting and unusual historical facts. We also have games and contests in class, which make it fun. After history I have typing. I used to think that typing was just for fun, but now I think it's an important skill to have. My teacher, Mr. Kankowsky, keeps telling us about all the different jobs we might someday have for which we'd need to be able to type. That makes the class more relevant. Fifth period is Glee Club. I had Glee Club in Phoenix, too, because I like to sing. Sometimes we sing during assemblies at school. We even get to sing at other schools sometimes. Everything about Glee Club is good.

My sixth-period class is gym. I like gym just as much as Glee Club. I like all sports, and I like my teacher, Mr. Coynes. Mr. Coynes is a pretty tough guy who doesn't take any back talk from anyone. I respect a person like that. That is what my classes are like this semester. I love some of them. But some—well . . . It's the good classes I have that make school worthwhile.

Getting Ready to Write

Soon you'll write a composition. In it you will describe your present classes. For the following activities, do your work on a separate sheet of paper.

I.

Your answers to the following items will form the introductory paragraph of your composition. Answer each item in a complete sentence. You may want to reread the first paragraph of Lynda Ryder's composition (page 90) before you begin.

    a. Give the name of your school.

    b. Tell the number of classes you have.

    c. Tell the number of classes you like and the number of classes you dislike, if any.

II.

Now plan the middle paragraphs of your composition. On your paper, draw boxes like those on pages 86–87.

    Draw one box for each of your classes. Label the boxes in order—first period, second period, third period, etc. In each box, jot down some notes about the subject of the class. Tell whether you like the subject and what happens in the class. When you write your composition, each box will become a separate paragraph.

III.

A composition should have a *concluding paragraph.* This paragraph summarizes and wraps up what you have already said. To plan your concluding paragraph, draw one more box on your paper. In the box, jot down some final thoughts about your classes. Reread the last paragraphs of "My Classes" (page 91) and "A Day in My Life" (above) before you begin writing your notes.

Class Writing

On a separate sheet of paper, write a composition in which you describe your present classes. Begin with the introductory paragraph you wrote for Part I on page 93. In your next five or six paragraphs, describe your classes—one class for each paragraph. Your last paragraph is your conclusion—a summary of what you have said in all the previous paragraphs.

Use your "Getting Ready to Write" notes to guide you. Also, use the compositions on pages 90–91 and 92–93 as models.

SKILL BUILDING

Commas and Conjunctions

Study the following complete sentences. Each has both a subject and a verb.

SUBJECT VERB SUBJECT VERB

Martha wore a cowboy hat to class. Nobody even noticed her.

By adding a **conjunction**—a word such as *and, but, so, yet,* or *or*—and a comma, we can join these two sentences into one.

COMMA CONJUNCTION

Martha wore a cowboy hat to class, but nobody even noticed her.

We no longer have two sentences. By being joined, each original sentence has been changed into what is called an independent clause. An **independent clause** is a sentence part that has both a subject and a verb and makes sense by itself.

INDEPENDENT CLAUSE   INDEPENDENT CLAUSE

Martha wore a cowboy hat to class, but nobody even noticed her.

I.

Five of the sentences that follow are made up of two independent clauses. The others are not. Read each sentence carefully. Then add a comma to each sentence that has two independent clauses. The other sentences do not need a comma.

EXAMPLES: (comma needed): Mr. Rinaldi is my science teacher, and he is also the coach of the track team.

(no comma needed): Mr. Rinaldi teaches science and coaches the track team.

1. Ms. Arnold teaches history and government but says she prefers to teach government.

2. I was in her history class last semester and I'm going to take her government class next semester.

3. Jeff said he was absent only once yet his report card says he was absent three times.

4. Last week Pat was tardy to class three days in a row so Mr. Mott sent her twice to detention.

5. She lives one block from our school but leaves her house late most of the time.

6. Mr. Steiner gives a math test once or twice each week.

7. He was out sick on Monday but he asked Mr. Chung-Loy to supervise the test.

8. Juan went home to get his assignment so he was late for class.

II.

Join the following pairs of sentences by using a comma and a conjunction *(and, or, so, yet,* or *but)*. Write each new sentence on the lines provided.

EXAMPLE: My dad is very good at math. Even he couldn't figure out the answer.
My dad is very good at math, yet even he couldn't figure out the answer.

1. Doug didn't do his homework. Mr. Bruner wanted to know why.

_____

_____

_____

2. I didn't know how to do the assignment. I called up my friend Janet and asked her how to do it.

_____

_____

_____

3. Mike never pays attention. That's why he's failing.

_____

_____

_____

4. I failed math last semester. This semester I'm getting an *A.*

_____

_____

_____

5. The class was almost over. I started getting my books together.

_____

_____

_____

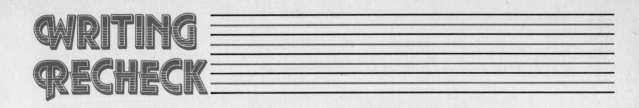
THINKING ABOUT WRITING

1. Look back at how you paragraphed your class-writing composition. Below, place a √ next to each item that tells how your writing is paragraphed.

   _____ My first paragraph is an introduction.

   _____ I then have five or six separate paragraphs, each of which deals with a different class.

   _____ My last paragraph is a conclusion. It wraps up what I have said.

   If you cannot put a check next to all of the items listed, rewrite your composition. When you are through, check your writing against the list again. Let your teacher know if you need help.

2. Have you given enough information in each of your paragraphs? On a separate sheet of paper, rewrite the third paragraph of your composition. Add two more sentences to it, giving a new detail about the class in each sentence.

SKILL BUILDING

3. Scan the composition by Lynda Ryder on pages 90–91. Underline all the sentences you can find that contain two independent clauses joined by a comma and a conjunction.

4. In your composition, do you have a sentence made up of two independent clauses joined by a comma and a conjunction? If so, circle the sentence(s). If not, find two related sentences in your composition that can be joined in this way. Write the one new sentence on your paper.

5. On your paper, write *one* sentence that gives the names of *all* the classes you have this term. Use commas to separate each name in the series.

ADVENTURE STORIES

Jungles are frightening places. They are filled with danger and mystery. For this reason, many good adventure stories are set in jungles. "King Solomon's Mines," "Leiningen versus the Ants," and "The Most Dangerous Game" are three exciting jungle stories you may already have read or would someday like to read.

For now, read "The Valley of the Statues." It is the story of a strange jungle valley that it's best not to visit.

The Valley of the Statues

Peter Munson moved along the green-canopied trail that led deep into the Malay jungle. A strong, stubborn man, he was undaunted by the searing heat and stinging insects. Nothing was going to stop him from finding the Valley of the Statues.

"I can't take it," a voice cried to him from behind.

Munson paused as Tollman, his partner, struggled to catch up. Gasping, the man collapsed near the foot of a tree. "I have to rest," Tollman muttered.

Munson scratched at his heavy blond beard. His steel-blue eyes fixed on Tollman. "We can't rest. You've slowed me down enough already."

"Just half an hour, 20 minutes."

"Listen," snapped Munson, "I've waited eight years for this expedition. Nineteen people, including my own father, have died—or disappeared—over the last decade while looking for the Valley of the Statues. With you or without you, I'm going to find it."

"Then go on without me," groaned Tollman. "I just can't take it."

"Done!" Munson growled. With a sneer, he turned and headed off down the trail.

An hour later he passed through a Senoi village. In Malay pidgin he asked a group of villagers about the Valley of the Statues. The people's eyes filled with fear.

The headman stepped forward. "There," he said, pointing across a range of hills. "But not go. You find, but you not return."

Briefly, Munson was afraid. He was not sure whether to go on. But a moment later his doubts turned into a renewed sense of purpose. He set off in the direction the headman had pointed.

He followed a path that led him down through a deep gorge. A dark, forboding jungle loomed ahead. Taking a deep breath, he pushed his way through thick vines and heavy foliage. His pace slackened. He began to feel strangely tired. His arms and legs felt heavy. His breath came in short gasps. But he continued on. He knew now he was near the Valley of the Statues.

Then there it was before him. In the jungle gloom stood hundreds of oddly lifelike statues. As he approached them his movements became leaden. His breathing became more labored. His mind seemed to be dulled.

He recognized one of the hardened faces. With one hand, he tried to reach, to touch, the face of his father. But to move the hand was now impossible. It had turned to stone.

Like so many before him, Munson had entered the Valley of the Statues. He had discovered its secret. And there he would remain forever.

THINKING ABOUT WHAT YOU HAVE READ

Answer in complete sentences.

1. In many stories there is a quest, or search, for something. For what was Munson searching, and why?

_____

_____

2. What are some of the clues indicating that the Valley of the Statues is very dangerous? Describe a specific passage in the story that gives one such clue. Be ready to discuss others.

_____

_____

_____

_____

3. What happens to Munson? And what has happened to all the others who entered the Valley?

_____

_____

4. What kind of man is Munson? Give a specific line from the story to support your answer. Be ready to point out others.

_____

_____

5. The *setting* of a story is where and when the action occurs. The setting greatly affects the action. What if "The Valley of the Statues" had been set in a desert in the year 2160? How might this setting change the details of the story's action? Explain your answer.

_____

_____

_____

_____

6. From what point of view is this story told? (To refresh your memory of point of view, you may turn back to page 78 of this book.)

_____

THINKING ABOUT WRITING

Paragraphing a Story

Like a factual composition, a short story must be divided into paragraphs. When you're writing, it is sometimes difficult to tell where one story paragraph should end and another begin. However, there are a few guidelines that can help story writers divide their work into paragraphs.

> In a story, begin a new paragraph when . . .
>
> - there is a shift in the action or the setting.
> - a character enters or leaves the scene.
> - a character begins speaking. Each *different* speaker gets a separate paragraph.

The following story has only 8 paragraphs when it should have 16. That is, each story paragraph is really two paragraphs run together. By drawing boxes, separate each paragraph into two, using the above guidelines. The first one has been done for you. (The story continues on page 102.)

The Invisible Tribe

Jacobs and I kept slashing our way through the jungle. We knew what we were looking for, but we had no idea if we were getting any closer to our goal. We came to a small clearing and sat down. After drinking thirstily from our canteens, we talked. Jacobs rehashed the stories of the "invisible tribe." I was too exhausted to listen. Besides, I had heard the stories a thousand times before.

Suddenly the jungle came alive. I jumped to my feet. I heard footsteps. I heard the sound of hundreds of bodies moving through the brush. "What is it?" whispered Jacobs, rising. He was trembling, and huge beads of sweat dripped from his brow.

"I don't know," I rasped. Jacobs gave me a terrified look. He grabbed my arm, and together we backed up, our eyes fixed on the jungle. It was in motion, as invisible bodies moved through it.

Suddenly the grass parted in front of us. Several sets of footprints moved across the ground. People seemed to be walking straight toward us, but we could see no one. A few moments later, I heard a voice. It said, "In the jungle one must be invisible. It is our only defense. Do you not agree?"

I looked at Jacobs. He looked at me. Neither of us knew what to say. We were both too scared to say anything. Then the voice began again. It said, "You may die. Or you may join us. The decision is yours. What do you wish to do?"

Both Jacobs and I certainly did not wish to die. We both stammered that we wanted to join them, whoever *they* were. An instant later I heard a hissing noise. Jacobs grabbed at his shoulder, as though he had been shot. Momentarily he vanished, right before my eyes.

And then I heard another hiss. I felt a terrible pain in my shoulder. I stared down at my shoulder. It was not there. Then I looked down at my body. It too was gone. "You have now joined the 'invisible tribe,' as you people call it," said the voice. "Follow me."

I heard Jacobs's voice. "They're the invisible tribe," he whined. Now we're one of them." I did not answer. I watched as footsteps retreated into the jungle. Numbly, I followed them.

Getting Ready to Write

Now get set to write a story about an adventure in a jungle. For the following activities, do your work on a separate sheet of paper.

I.

Follow the directions given in each numbered item.

1. In your story you will be looking for something in a jungle. You will be on a quest. Which of the following do you think would be most interesting to pursue? Write it on your paper.
   a. gorillas that have the minds of humans
   b. a pond that makes old people young again
   c. a mountain that keeps growing taller as you climb it
   d. Martians who have set up a colony in a jungle
   e. creatures that have human heads and crocodile bodies
   f. other (Write a choice of your own if you prefer.)

2. You will write your story from the first-person point of view. (See page 78.) There will be one other character in the story. This character will be your companion in the jungle. Write the name of this person on your paper.

II.

Now you know the object of your search and your story characters. The next step is to plan the action and the other details. First, on your paper, draw eight boxes like the one that follows.

The boxes stand for paragraphs in your story. Number the boxes in order, from 1 through 8. Then, in the boxes, jot down the information called for in the following list.

Box 1: Describe who you are, who is with you, and where the two of you are. Explain what you are looking for.

Box 2: Describe the jungle. Tell what it is like to make your way—or cut your way—through it.

Box 3: You and your companion get tired and sit down to rest. Where do you sit down? What do you say to your companion? Jot down some ideas.

Box 4: You begin to walk again. Suddenly something scares you. What is it? Make it something related to the thing you are looking for. (For example, in "The Invisible Tribe," Jacobs and the narrator are frightened by footsteps and the sounds of "hundreds of bodies moving through the brush.")

Box 5: You find the thing you have been looking for. What does it look like? What does it do? What, if anything, does it say?

Box 6: What do you and your companion do in response? Do you laugh? Do you become frightened? Do you run toward the thing or away from it?

Box 7: What happens next to you and your companion? (For example, do you turn into gorillas with human minds?) Jot down this second-to-last step in the action.

Box 8: How does your adventure end? (For example, do you walk off with other gorillas with human minds? Do you mysteriously escape from the jungle?) Be sure to tie up all the loose ends of your story.

Writing an Adventure Story

On a separate sheet of paper, write your adventure story. Be sure to divide it into paragraphs. Use the worksheet you made for "Getting Ready to Write" to guide you.

The writing you are about to do will be a first draft only. When you finish the "Writing Recheck" (page 105), you will make a final, corrected copy of your adventure story.

SKILL BUILDING

Commas and Subordinate Clauses

Like an independent clause, a *subordinate clause* has both a subject and a verb. But a subordinate clause cannot stand alone as a sentence. This is because it begins with words such as *if, while, since, because, so that, though,* or *although,* and it does not express a complete thought. A subordinate clause must be joined to an independent clause in order to complete its meaning.

SUBJECT VERB

Though it is not a well-known fact,   the Sahara Desert was once a jungle.

SUBORDINATE CLAUSE   INDEPENDENT CLAUSE

As you see in the example, a comma is used after the subordinate clause when it comes first in the sentence.

Match the clauses to form sentences that make sense. Write a letter in the blank before each numeral. Then, on a separate sheet of paper, write each new, complete sentence. Place the subordinate clause at the beginning.

SUBORDINATE CLAUSES   INDEPENDENT CLAUSES

_____ 1. So that the dead will feel at home,

_____ 2. While on a trip into the jungles of Brazil,

_____ 3. Because it has eyes on the sides of its head,

_____ 4. Though the Amazon is one of the world's major rivers,

_____ 5. If a man of the Somba tribe wishes to marry a woman,

_____ 6. Though the children of New Guinea are almost always blond,

_____ 7. After the death of African king Kokodo,

_____ 8. Although the Australian aborigines do not mind being seen without garments,

a. the African jerboa can see behind it without turning its head.

b. no one knows exactly where it begins.

c. he must work for her family eight years without pay before they can be wed.

d. two workers discovered a tribe of fair-skinned, red-haired people.

e. graves in the jungle areas of Sierra Leone are covered by thatched roofs.

f. being seen eating embarrasses them greatly.

g. his body was moved around in a square coffin on wheels.

h. they become dark haired as they grow older.

THINKING ABOUT WRITING

1. If you did not give your adventure story a title, do so now. Write it at the top of your paper. If your story already has a title, see if you can think of a better one.

2. Exchange stories with one of your classmates. Give your classmate two letter grades. The first is for how interesting the story is. The second is for how well the story has been broken into paragraphs. Then discuss together all changes and corrections that will make each story better.

3. Do any sentences in your story include many words when a single word would work just as well? If so, rewrite such sentences on the following blank lines. Underline the one word that takes the place of many. Reread Lesson 6, pages 42–48, before you begin this activity.

_____

_____

_____

_____

_____

SKILL BUILDING

4. Look through your adventure story for a sentence with a subordinate clause before an independent clause. If you find one, underline it. If you do not find one, make one up that would be appropriate for your story. Make sure you put a comma after the subordinate clause.

5. Study your use of commas in your story. Have you left any out that are needed? Have you used any that do not belong? Make whatever corrections are necessary. (Ask your teacher for help if you have questions.)

6. Check the paragraphs in your story against the items that follow.

   a. Did you begin a new paragraph each time there is a shift in the action or the setting?
   b. Did you begin a new paragraph each time a character enters or leaves the scene?
   c. Did you begin a new paragraph each time a character begins to speak?

   Now make a final, clean copy of your story. As you do, be sure to make all the paragraph changes and all the other corrections that are needed. You may wish to reread the "Thinking about Writing" on page 101 before you begin.

JOBS AND INTERVIEWS

What is it like to be a beautician, a truck driver, or a police officer? What are the good points of each job? What are the bad points? What sort of education does each job require?

Most adults are eager to talk about their work. It is a very important part of their lives. They usually want people to understand and appreciate what they go through each day on the job.

Barbara Tani of Toledo, Ohio, interviewed her father about his work. She took notes as he talked. Then, based on her notes, she wrote the following composition.

My Father's Work

I conducted an interview with my father, Dr. James Tani. My father is a dentist. He is 43 years old. He has been a dentist for 18 years.

To become a dentist my dad had to have a lot of schooling. After graduating from high school, he didn't know what he wanted to do. In his own words, he "bummed around for about a year." Then he enrolled in college, at Ohio State. At first he was going to be a psychologist. Then he decided to be a dentist. After four years he got his Bachelor of Science degree. Then he went to dental school and earned his D.D.S. (Doctor of Dental Surgery).

If you have been to a dentist, you have some idea of what my dad does. He examines teeth. He drills cavities and puts in fillings. He caps teeth, crowns them, and does root canals. Sometimes he has to pull teeth. He also tells his patients what they can do to take better care of their teeth.

There are a number of things about my dad's job that he doesn't like. Drilling and using a needle to inject novocaine can hurt people, and he doesn't like to cause pain. Also, the mouth is very small, making it a difficult thing to work on. Both he and the patient are in awkward positions. Both are tense and uncomfortable. Some people complain a lot and squirm around. Some close their mouths down on my dad's fingers. That just makes the job a lot harder for him.

But there are also many things my dad likes about his job. Some of the patients are fun to talk with. My dad likes to joke with them and learn about their lives. Also, the hours are not bad, and the pay is good. However, the feeling that he is helping people is what my dad likes best. He makes his patients look better and feel better. He says that that makes him proud of the work he does.

I asked my dad if there is one thing that happened on the job that he will always remember. He thought for a minute. Then he laughed. He told me that one day a big strong man came into his office. The man had three cavities. He sat down in the chair and said, "Okay, Doc, let's get on with it." My dad got ready to give the man a shot of novocaine. The man saw the needle, shook his head, and ran right out of the office!

Interviewing my dad was a lot of fun. Of course, I knew he was a dentist, but I didn't know much about what dentistry is like. I learned a great deal about what he has to go through every day. I also learned how much his work means to him. He seemed really pleased to have a chance to tell me about himself and his job. And I was glad that I'd finally asked.

THINKING ABOUT WHAT YOU HAVE READ

Answer in complete sentences.

1. Had Dr. Tani always wanted to be a dentist? Give a detail from the composition to support your answer.

_____

_____

_____

_____

2. What are *two* things Dr. Tani does not like about his work?

_____

_____

_____

_____

3. What is the *one* thing he likes most?

_____

_____

_____

_____

4. Why did Barbara enjoy interviewing her dad?

_____

_____

_____

5. Why did her dad enjoy being interviewed?

_____

_____

_____

THINKING ABOUT WRITING

The Interview—Organizing Information

In an interview, the person to whom you are talking may not always give you the information you want in the order in which you plan to use it. For instance, the person may change the subject, ramble on about something else, and then come back to the subject. You may ask a question for which he or she has no immediate answer. Then a few minutes later, in the middle of talking about something else, the person may suddenly think of an answer to your earlier question.

Meanwhile, you are trying to take notes. You can't write as fast as the person is talking. You never get some things down on paper. Others get noted in the wrong places, perhaps scribbled in a margin.

Later you have to write a composition based on your notes. They are jumbled and messy. The first step you have to take before you begin to put your interview into writing is to get your notes organized.

Following are notes from an interview with a history teacher about her job. First, read all the information. Then go on to the activities that follow.

_____ 1. good hours—only works from 8 to 3

_____ 2. likes the kids—likes helping them and seeing them improve

_____ 3. bothers her to see kids who ditch school or who don't work at school—most of them will be failures

_____ 4. has to take attendance

_____ 5. has to make sure the room is neat—heater is working—things are organized

_____ 6. likes to joke with the kids—"they can be fun to joke with and talk with"

_____ 7. went to college, Michigan State, for four years to get B.A. (Bachelor of Arts) degree—another year beyond that to get teaching credential

_____ 8. "pay is low—considering the amount of education the job takes, how hard it can be, and how important it is"

_____ 9. doesn't like doing all the paperwork and dislikes waste of class time spent doing things other than teaching

_____ 10. must continue her own education in order to get adequate pay raises

_____ **11.** talks only part of the period (If you talk too much, she says, the kids get bored.), gives assignments, goes around and helps kids, gives tests and corrects them

_____ **12.** likes her subject, which is history (makes the job nicer if you like what you're teaching)

_____ **13.** has been teaching for nine years—one year at Taft Jr. High, eight at Ward Jr. High

_____ **14.** doesn't like to have to put up with kids who come in late, interrupt her when she's talking, or fool around in class

_____ **15.** likes the job because she likes being around kids

_____ **16.** taking summer courses to get her master's degree in history

_____ **17.** her name: Vera Dietz—my aunt; 33 years old

_____ **18.** says, "a teacher is largely her own boss, and I like being my own boss"

_____ **19.** doesn't like to have to grade papers at home—doesn't like a job she has to take home with her

_____ **20.** liked being interviewed—said it was nice to get a chance to talk about her work, though at first she didn't seem as though she would like it

_____ **21.** has to prepare lessons and then give them

_____ **22.** interview gave my aunt a chance to tell her side of things—something she thinks students should know

_____ **23.** will always remember the blind student who wanted to be in her class (He listened closely in class and read the history book in Braille. He typed his work.)

_____ **24.** I thanked my aunt and told her I enjoyed interviewing her. It was fun seeing her side of things.

_____ **25.** blind student was Bryan Dunwald—was one of the nicest kids she'd ever taught (gave her a present of perfume on last day of school)

I.

Organize the list of notes you just read. Using the following directions, write a letter in the blank before each numbered note.

A. The first, or introductory, paragraph of the interview composition would give the following facts: the person's name, age, job, and length of time in the job. Look over the notes from the interview with history teacher Vera Dietz. Write the letter **A** next to each item you would use in the introductory paragraph.

B. Which items tell about the education Ms. Dietz needed in order to become a teacher? Which tell about her continuing education? Write the letter **B** next to each of these items.

C. Which items tell what the teacher has to do on the job? Write **C** next to each of these items.

D. Which items tell about things the teacher dislikes? Write **D** next to them.

E. Which items tell about the things Ms. Dietz likes about her job? Write **E** next to them.

F. Which items tell about something special she remembers from her job? Write **F** next to them.

G. Which items would make a good conclusion? Which items tell how both persons felt about the interview after it was over? Which items tell what they got out of the interview? Write **G** next to these items.

II.

Suppose you were going to write a composition based on the interview with Vera Dietz. The list of notes contains a great deal of information. You would want to choose the most important and interesting information and leave out the rest.

Complete this step now. Study the list of interview notes. Draw two lines under all the items you would definitely include in the composition. Draw one line under the items you _might_ include. Cross out the items you definitely would not include. Be ready to explain your choices.

Getting Ready to Write

Soon you will write a composition that describes the job of an adult you have interviewed. You will need to complete the following activities before you begin writing.

I.

Choose an adult you would like to interview. The adult may be a parent, another relative, or a friend. First, on a separate sheet of paper, write this person's name, age, and job. Then ask each of the following questions. Take notes as the person answers.

1. How long have you been doing your present job?

2. What kind of education, training, or other experiences did you need in order to get and to keep your job?

3. What do you do in your job? What are some of the things you do during a typical day?

4. What, if anything, do you dislike about your job?

5. What do you like about your job?

6. Is there something that happened while you were doing your job that you will always remember? If there is, please describe the incident.

   (Question 7 is missing. On the lines provided, write one question of your own. Be sure to ask this question during the interview.)

7. _____

   _____

   _____

   _____

8. Did you enjoy being interviewed about your job? Please explain why you did or did not.

   Now you, the interviewer, should write why you did or did not enjoy doing the interview.

II.

Look over your notes. Draw two lines under the items of information you will definitely include in your composition. Draw one line under the items you *might* include. Cross out the items you definitely will not include.

Interview Writing

On a separate sheet of paper, write the first draft of a composition based on your interview of an adult. Use the notes you made in "Getting Ready to Write" (page 112) as your source of information.

Plan to write eight paragraphs, as follows:
1. introduction (Give the name, age, job, and length of time in the job of the person you interviewed.)
2. education or training needed to obtain and to do the job
3. what the person does each day on the job
4. what the person dislikes about the job
5. what the person likes about the job
6. a memorable on-the-job experience
7. additional information (Base this paragraph on the person's response to item 7 on page 112.)
8. conclusion (Tell how you and the person felt about the interview.)

You may use Barbara Tani's composition (pages 106–107) as a model. When you've finished writing your first draft, wait for your teacher's instructions.

SKILL BUILDING

Commas and "Add-ons"

Commas are used to set off many "added-on" words and phrases. Words and phrases such as *therefore, to begin with, however, for example, interestingly, secondly,* and *in addition* can be inserted at the beginning, middle, or end of many sentences. Notice where the commas are placed in the three sentences that follow.

For example, John has worked here only one month.
John, for example, has worked here only one month.
John has worked here only one month, for example.

I.

Find the "added-on" words and phrases in the following sentences. Set them off with commas. (Use two commas when the word or phrase is in the middle of the sentence.) The first one has been done for you.

1. Thus, Julie Nixon Eisenhower became an editor for the *Saturday Evening Post.*

2. For example Marilyn Monroe once worked in a factory.

3. The first understandable words transmitted by telephone on the other hand were spoken by Alexander Graham Bell in 1876.

4. George Harrison soon discovered however that he was not suited to be an electrician.

5. Paul Laurence Dunbar believe it or not was working as an elevator operator when his first volume of poems was published.

6. Interestingly Benito Mussolini was once an elementary-school teacher.

7. Furthermore Gene Hackman entered the working world as a Times Square doorman.

8. Crystal Gayle's father of course was a coal miner.

9. Mark Hammill in the meantime landed a role on the soap opera "General Hospital."

10. People like Ron Howard literally grew up on television for example.

II.

Fill in the blanks in each item to form a complete sentence. Write one word in each blank. Various "add-on" words and phrases are already included. Be sure to set off these "add-on" words or phrases with commas. (If the word or phrase is at the beginning or the end of the sentence, use one comma. If it is inside the sentence, use two commas.)

EXAMPLE:

Furthermore, *that* *was* *not* *really* *fair*.

1. Therefore _____ _____ _____ _____

_____ _____.

2. Believe it or not _____ _____ _____

_____ _____ _____ _____.

3. _____ _____ on the other hand _____

_____ _____ _____ _____.

4. Also _____ _____ _____ _____.

5. As you know _____ _____ _____ _____

_____ _____ for example.

114

THINKING ABOUT WRITING

1. Did you give your "interview writing" a title? If not, do so now.

2. Sometimes writers try to "say" too much. Is this the case anywhere in your writing? Do any of your paragraphs have sentences that give details that are not important or not interesting? If so, cross out these sentences.

3. Study the paragraphs of your composition, one by one. Underline each topic sentence. (Add a topic sentence to any paragraph that lacks one.) Check that every sentence in the paragraph gives information about the main idea stated in the topic sentence. Cross out sentences that give unrelated details.

SKILL BUILDING

4. Find one sentence in the composition by Barbara Tani (pages 106–107) that uses commas to set off a series of actions. Underline it.

5. Be sure that you've used commas correctly to set off any "add-ons" in your composition. Then check for commas in the following cases: in a series of nouns (page 80), in a series of actions (page 80), with a conjunction between independent clauses (pages 94–95), between a subordinate and an independent clause (page 104). The page numbers in parentheses ( ) tell you where to look to review each rule.

6. Now give your composition one final check. Take a close look at how you paragraphed your writing. Be sure you've made all the changes and corrections that are needed, and that you have the best composition possible. Then make a clean copy of your composition. Reread it for copying errors.

PLAY WRITING

Plays and life have something in common. Both are full of characters. You may have seen some of the characters in the following play.

Har Har Har

CHARACTERS: Narrator   Ms. Lotta Lernen
                     Justin Sane   Sigfried Uncker
                     Norman Normal Avery Fakeman

SCENE I

NARRATOR: We are in Ms. Lotta Lernen's period-five history class. Class has already begun. Ms. Lernen is sitting at her desk, talking to the class.

MS. L: Today, class, I want to begin by making sure that you all read chapters one and two in the history book last night. I'm going to call on you and ask you some questions. Now for my first question. (*points to* Justin Sane). Leif Eriksson is believed to have been the first European to visit America. Justin, what did he name it?

JUSTIN: Huh? I don't know. Uh, Disneyland? Har har har.

MS. L (*shakes her head in annoyance*): Be serious, Justin. That is incorrect. (*She looks around the room. She points to* Norman Normal.) Norman, do you know the answer?

NORMAN: I think so. I think Eriksson called it Vinland, or "Wineland." He named it that because of all the grapes growing where he landed.

MS. L: Good! That is correct. Thank you.

JUSTIN (*to* Norman): Show-off! Har har. Teacher's pet.

MS. L: Did you hear what Norman said, Justin?

JUSTIN: Har har. Did he say something?

MS. L: Justin, did you even read the assignment last night?

JUSTIN (*turns to his pal* Sigfried): Did we have an assignment last night? Har har. I don't think so. Har har har.

SIGFRIED: What's an assignment? Erk erk erk.

MS. L: History is very important; learning is very important. Your whole future depends on what you know.

JUSTIN: Golly, I didn't know that. Har har har.
MS. L: Learning always pays off, sooner or later.
JUSTIN: Probably right, but I got better things to do. (*He puts his head on his desk and is soon in dreamland. Now and then he giggles in his sleep.*)

SCENE II

NARRATOR: It is later in the same afternoon. We are in the home of Justin Sane. He is with his buddy Sigfried Uncker.
JUSTIN: Flip on the tube, dude.

SIGFRIED (*turns on the TV set and watches the picture come on*): Oh, radical! It's "National Phono-Quiz."

NARRATOR: They watch as Avery Fakeman comes hopping happily onto the stage.

AVERY: Hey! Hi, everybody! It's time to play "Phono-Quiz." Time to roll those ol' magic phone dials. And if your number comes up, hey, hey, hey . . . It's automatic dialing time, straight to your home. We lay the big question on you. And if you know the answer, it's a million buckeroos for you!

JUSTIN (*to TV*): Roll it, dude.

AVERY: Yeh, hey, let's roll. (*He rolls ten huge phone dials of numbers.*) Hey, hey, hey. We've got a zero, a nine, a four, a zero, a seven, a one, a four, a five, a nine, and a four.

JUSTIN: That's my number!

AVERY: Our magic number is ringing right now somewhere.

(Justin's *phone rings. He nervously picks up the receiver.*)

JUSTIN: Ah, hewwo.

AVERY: Hey, hey, hey. Avery Fakeman here. Is this (094) 071—4594?

JUSTIN: Uh, uh-huh. Uh, yup 'tis.

AVERY: And who am I speaking to?

JUSTIN (*to Sigfried*): Who's he speaking to?

SIGFRIED: You, dingbat!

JUSTIN (*into phone*): To me. You're talking to me. I'm Justin Sane.

AVERY: Hey, fer sure, fer sure. Okay, Justin. For one million bucks, answer this question! (*pause*) Leif Eriksson, who was the first European to visit America, gave it another name. Justin, for the chance of a lifetime, what name did Leif give America?

JUSTIN: Duh. Uh. I had that question today. Uh. I don't know. Let's see. Uh. What was it? I didn't read my . . .

AVERY: Two seconds . . .

JUSTIN: Ah, nuts, man.

AVERY (*a gong sounds*): I'm sorry, Justin, but it was not Nutsman. You're our big loser for today! Bye bye.

(Justin's *chin begins quivering, and he starts to cry.*)

AVERY: And now we will call our second number. (*He spins the dials.*) A zero, a nine, a four, a zero, an eight, a one, a two, a two, a four, and a nine. And the phone is ringing. Someone is answering.

NORMAN: Hello, Norman Normal speaking

AVERY: Hey, hey, hey. Hiya, Norm. Have you been watching "Phono-Quiz"? Have you heard our question?

JUSTIN (*stares at TV in disbelief*): Oh, no, it's him!

NORMAN: Yes, I've heard the question. And the answer is Vinland. Leif Eriksson called America Vinland.

AVERY: Wooooooooow! Right you are! You're filthy rich! Hey, hey, hey, what've you got to say?

NORMAN: I'm really excited. . . . Really happy . . .

AVERY: Anything else? Do you want to say anything to all the folks watching out there in televisiondom?

NORMAN: Well, I would like to say something to your last contestant.

AVERY: And what's that?

NORMAN: Har har har!

THINKING ABOUT WHAT YOU HAVE READ

Answer in complete sentences.

1. Have you ever known or heard of anyone like Justin Sane? Briefly describe this person.

   _____

   _____

   _____

   _____

2. In your opinion, what kind of person is Avery Fakeman? Have you ever known or seen someone like him? Include details in your answers.

   _____

   _____

   _____

   _____

3. What do you think are some of the funniest lines in the play? What is the funniest thing that happens? Give reasons for your answers.

   _____

   _____

   _____

   _____

   _____

4. Though "Har Har Har" is a comedy, it has a point to make. It has a theme: learning pays off. Do you agree? Do you believe that learning pays? Explain your answer.

   _____

   _____

   _____

   _____

   _____

Thinking About Writing

Understanding Characterization and Purpose

People's speech reveals much about them. Their choices of words, their accents, and the subjects they choose to talk about most often indicate something about the speakers.

In a play, a writer has only the characters' words and a few stage directions to use in telling a story. The writer can tell us very little about the characters in a direct way. Instead, writers must create *dialogue,* characters' spoken words, that will give as much information as possible about the characters.

I.

Read the following sentences from "Har Har Har." Then, on the lines, explain what each sentence tells you about the character who is speaking.

1. SIGFRIED UNCKER: What's an assignment? Erk erk erk. (page 116)

   _____

   _____

2. MS. LOTTA LERNEN: History is very important; learning is very important. (page 116)

   _____

   _____

3. JUSTIN SANE: Golly, I didn't know that. Har har har. (page 117)

   _____

   _____

4. AVERY FAKEMAN: And if you know the answer, it's a million buckeroos for you! (page 118)

   _____

   _____

5. NORMAN NORMAL: Well, I would like to say something to your last contestant. (page 118)

   _____

   _____

Spoken language, when combined with actors' movements and expressions, brings a play to life on the stage. The writer of a play often wants the dialogue to be as lifelike as possible. Yet in real life, people do not speak perfectly. They use sentence fragments. Sometimes they use the wrong word or let a sentence run on and on.

Because the speech in a play is usually written to sound like real speech, it can contain "errors" that writers are taught to avoid. The point is that every kind of writing has its own purpose. You would not write dialogue for a play, for example, in the same way that you would write a business letter or a report for school.

II.

On the lines, rewrite each sentence that follows as it might be spoken by the given character. Your purpose is to make the dialogue sound lifelike. Review "Har Har Har," on pages 116 through 118, before you begin.

EXAMPLE: JUSTIN SANE: You are probably correct, but I have more important interests.

Probably right, but I got better things to do.

1. JUSTIN SANE: I do not have any interest in history.

   _____

   _____

2. AVERY FAKEMAN: I sincerely hope you will watch our show tomorrow.

   _____

   _____

3. LOTTA LERNEN: Learning always provides great benefits.

   _____

   _____

4. SIGFRIED UNCKER: I failed my history exam, Justin.

   _____

   _____

5. NORMAN NORMAL: This is a moment of great excitement for me.

   _____

   _____

III.

Look back at "Har Har Har," on pages 116 through 118. From the dialogue, choose *five* sentences that contain words that would *not* be appropriate for formal writing. On a separate sheet of paper, rewrite each sentence so that it contains none of those inappropriate words.

Getting Ready to Write

On pages 123 through 124 you will write the dialogue for a play. The following activities will help you get ready to write.

I.

On a separate sheet of paper, answer each of the following questions in complete sentences. Base your answers on your experience in the classroom.

1. Do students behave differently when they have a substitute teacher? Give details to explain your answer.

2. Imagine a student getting up and sharpening a pencil while the teacher is talking. What would the teacher probably do and say?

3. What might a teacher say to a student who is late for class?

4. What excuse might the tardy student give in response?

II.

Read the directions for the play-writing activity on page 123. Read through the play in its entirety to get a feel for what happens.

III.

The *climax*, or turning point, of the play is left blank. We know that Ramar Phooey is a magician. Therefore, he is going to use his magic skills! Below, jot down some ideas about what he might do.

_____

_____

_____

_____

_____

Play Writing

The narrative portion of a short play follows. The dialogue has been left out. First, read the whole narrative carefully to be sure you understand the story. Then, on the lines, write the words the characters are saying. Finally, add an ending to the play. Write your ending on the lines provided.

Use your answers to "Getting Ready to Write" (page 122) to guide you.

Ramar's Revenge

NARRATOR: It is 8:00 A.M. in Ms. Beverly Hill's science class. Ms. Hill is absent, and Mr. Ramar Phooey is filling in. Mr. Phooey is a magician, temporarily employed as a substitute teacher. The students are noisy and rowdy. Mr. Phooey steps in front of the class.

MR. RP: _____

SHEILA (*to* Irene): _____

IRENE (*to* Sheila): _____

MIKE (*yelling across the room to* Debbie): _____

_____

DEBBIE (*answering* Mike): _____

_____

MR. RP: _____

MIKE (*to* Mr. RP): _____

IRENE (*to* Mike): _____

MIKE: _____

(Doug *walks to the pencil sharpener.*)

MR. RP (*to* Doug): _____

DOUG: _____

(Doug *sharpens his pencil, then ambles back to his seat.*)

MR. RP (*to* Doug): _____

DOUG: _____

(Terry, Gracie, *and* Brian *come in late.*)

TERRY (*looking at* Mr. RP): _____

123

GRACIE (*laughing*): _____

BRIAN: _____

MR. RP (*to the three tardy students*): _____

_____

BRIAN: _____

TERRY: _____

(*The whole class laughs. Mr. RP gets more and more angry.*)

SHEILA (*to Mr. RP*): _____

MR. RP: _____

MIKE (*to Mr. RP*): _____

(*Mr. RP is furious. His eyes begin to glow like two silver disks.*)

MR. RP (*to class*): _____

_____

_____

BRIAN (*to Mr. RP*): _____

_____

MR. RP: _____

_____

_____

(*Mr. RP raises his hands and mumbles strange words. The class begins to get frightened.*)

SHEILA: _____

IRENE: _____

MIKE: _____

(*Mr. RP closes his eyes, then claps his hands together. Sparks fly from his fingertips. The students in the class begin to glow. Suddenly . . .*)

_____

_____

_____

SKILL BUILDING

Commas and Names

Commas are used to set off the name of a person being spoken to.

Martin, she's leaving now!
I explained it, Martin, but you weren't listening.
Do you know the answer, Martin?

No commas are used when the person is being spoken about.

Martin is weird.
Not many people want Martin for a friend.

I.

The following sentences all have *Tom* in them. Some of the sentences are about him. In others, he is being spoken to. Don't add any commas to those sentences that are about Tom. But *do* add commas to those in which he is being spoken to. Eight commas are needed in all.

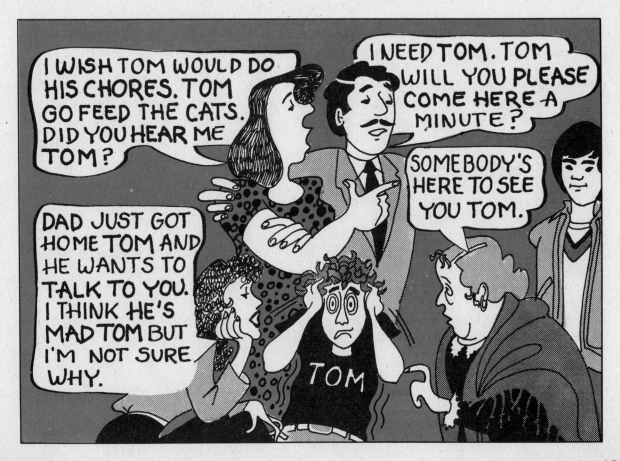

II.

Follow the directions given. Do your work on a separate sheet of paper.

1. Write 15 sentences in which you are *speaking to,* or addressing, someone named Mary. In sentences 1 through 5, write her name, then a comma, at the beginning. In sentences 6 through 10, write her name at the end of the sentence, and add a comma before the name. In sentences 11 through 15, put her name in the middle, and add a comma before and after it.

   EXAMPLES: Mary, will you change the station?
   I really like you, Mary.
   I will help you, Mary, but not for long.

2. Write five sentences *about* Mary. No commas are needed either before or after her name.

THINKING ABOUT WRITING

1. Exchange the play you wrote on pages 123 through 124 with a classmate. Compare what was said and how it was said. Compare endings. Then talk with your classmate about changes each of you might want to make.

2. On your own paper, rewrite the first four lines of your play. Create new dialogue that makes each character into a different kind of person with a different way of speaking.

3. Imagine that Mr. Ramar Phooey is from a part of the U.S. whose people have a distinctive way of speaking, or a way of speaking that is different from the one heard where you live. On your paper, rewrite one of Ramar's lines to show this difference in speech.

SKILL BUILDING

4. Did you use commas to set off the names of persons being spoken to in your dialogue? Study your play carefully. Add commas where they are needed.

5. Check your end-of-sentence punctuation. Make sure that you use exclamation points (!) for sentences expressing anger or surprise. For all questions, use a question mark. End the remaining sentences with periods.

6. A sentence is incomplete it if lacks a subject, a verb, or both. It is acceptable to use incomplete sentences, or *fragments,* when writing dialogue, because in real life, people sometimes speak in fragments.

   EXAMPLE: SUE: Where to now?   JOE: Home.

   Put a √ next to each sentence fragment in your play. Then, on a separate sheet of paper, rewrite each one as a complete sentence.

WRITING A REPORT

The development of modern Mexico, the building of the Brooklyn Bridge, the invention of trousers: these report topics can be very interesting. There are many fascinating facts to be learned about each of them.

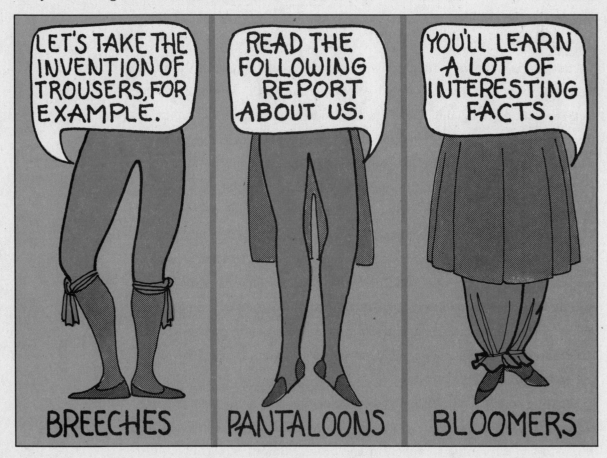

The Pants Invention

Trousers were invented in prehistoric times by people who lived in cold northern climates. The garment provided good protection against the cold. Both men and women wore it.

At first, people who wore trousers were thought of as barbarians. Roman and Greek men wore skirts. They made fun of anyone who wore trousers.

Little by little, trousers started becoming popular among people in other parts of the world. Believe it or not, the horse was the cause of this popularity. Skirts, robes, and dresses were not well suited to horseback riding, while trousers were. Then, because men spent more time riding than did women, trousers slowly became a garment for men. Skirts and dresses became garments for women.

Early trousers were not like those of today. Known as breeches, they reached to just below the knee. With breeches, knee-high socks were worn. Most early breeches were made of leather. Not until the nineteenth century did cloth ones come into use.

Today the word *trousers* has an old-fashioned sound. Many people use the word *pants* instead. *Pants* is an abbreviated form of *pantaloons,* a word that comes from "Pantalone," the name of a character in an Italian play of many centuries ago.

Pantaloons were very tight trousers worn especially during the nineteenth century. Usually they were strapped either to the ankles or to the feet. For a time in England, it was the style to wear pantaloons so tight that the wearer almost could not get into them. Special pegs were invented over which the pantaloons could be stretched and held open. The man then climbed up on a ladder and literally jumped into his pants! This was the only way he could get them on.

Until the nineteenth century, it was a strict rule of dress that men should wear pants and women should wear skirts and dresses. In 1851 a woman named Amelia Bloomer changed this "rule." Miss Bloomer caused a sensation by appearing in public in loose-fitting pants. Soon many women were following her example. Though there was a great public outcry against "bloomers," as this garment came to be called, a new era in women's clothing had begun.

Today, of course, it is completely acceptable for women to wear pants. A corresponding change in men's clothing, however, has not taken place. But who's to say what might happen in the future? Someday, perhaps, most men will wear skirts and robes, as the ancient Greeks and Romans did, while men who continue to wear pants will be thought of as crude, old-fashioned barbarians!

Bibliography

Encyclopaedia Britannica, Vol. 7, pp. 675–689, Chicago, Encyclopaedia Britannica, Inc., 1970.

Garrison, Webb, *How It Started*, New York, Abingdon Press, 1972.

Morris, William, *Dictionary of Word and Phrase Origins*, New York, Harper and Row, 1962.

THINKING ABOUT WHAT YOU HAVE READ

Answer in complete sentences.

1. What did the men in ancient Greece and Rome wear instead of trousers?

    _____

    _____

2. How did the word *pants* come into being?

    _____

    _____

3. Did women wear trousers at any time before the nineteenth century? If so, how and why did women's clothing styles change?

    _____

    _____

    _____

    _____

4. Did you find the report interesting? Was it worthwhile both to write and to read? Explain your answers, using details from the report.

    _____

    _____

    _____

    _____

    _____

Thinking About Writing

Researching a Topic

Writing a report is something every student has to do a number of times during his or her school career. Many students, of course, groan, when asked to do so.

But there really is no reason to groan. In fact, writing a report can be truly fun and interesting. The first step is to have something to say. After choosing a subject, find as many interesting facts and bits of information on the subject as you can. Next, organize your ideas. Then put all you have learned into a structured piece of writing. Believe it or not, the whole process can be very rewarding.

Before you work through the steps in report writing one at a time, it's important to know how to locate the information you will need. The *encyclopedia* is an essential tool for report writers. It contains articles, arranged in alphabetical order, on many hundreds of different subjects.

Study the following illustration of a set of encyclopedia. Use it in answering the numbered items.

Following are some general report topics. On the line after each, write the number of the encyclopedia volume in which you would find information about that topic. For those items that have more than one topic, you will need to list more than one volume number. The first item has been done for you.

1. Guatemala   _8_

2. The Typewriter   _____

3. The Black Sea   _____

4. George "Babe" Ruth   _____

5. Badminton and Ping-Pong   _____

6. The Sari   _____

7. Joe Louis and Jack Dempsey   _____

8. Nevada   _____   12. Danzig   _____

9. India and Portugal   _____   13. The Nile, Amazon, and
                                                    Mississippi rivers   _____
10. Charles Darwin   _____
                                                14. Snakes   _____
11. The Sewing Machine   _____

Getting Ready to Write

Soon you are going to write a report. The following activities will help you to get ready. For Parts II through VI, do your work on a separate sheet of paper.

I.

Choose and underline the *one* topic in the following list that you would most like to write about. Or, if the topic of your choice is not listed, write a topic on the line provided.

1. The First Olympic Games   6. Modern Motorcycles
2. The History of Bowling   7. The Invention of Television
3. Customs of the Apache People   8. Betsy Ross
4. The War of 1812   9. Ulysses S. Grant
5. Harriet Tubman   10. Amelia Jenks Bloomer

(Other) _____

II.

The next step is to ask yourself some good questions about your topic. These should be the questions a reader would most want to have answered. Write your questions—at least five but no more than eight—on your paper.

EXAMPLE: *Topic*—The First Olympic Games
            1. When and where did the Olympic Games begin?
            2. Why were the Olympic Games started?
            3. Who took part in the first games?
            4. Which sports were included, and how were the winners honored?
            5. What were the first games like?
            6. Were the first Olympic Games as popular as the Olympics of today?

III.

Now plan the paragraphs of your report. On your paper, draw one box for each of the questions you wrote in Part II. Then copy one question above each box.

IV.

Now gather facts and details to answer each question. Begin by looking up your topic in an encyclopedia. Find the most important and interesting information that best helps to answer each question. In your own words, write this information in the box under the appropriate question. Next, go to at least one more reference work, a book, or a magazine article. If possible, check the facts you've already noted in each box. Then, in your own words, write any new information you think should be added to each box.

V.

At the end of your written notes, be sure to write the following information about the references you used. Place a comma after each piece of information within each item.

1. *For encyclopedias:* Give the full name of the encyclopedia (underlined), the volume number(s) in which you found the information, and the page number. Then list the place of publication, the name of the publishing company, and the year of publication.
2. *For other books:* Give the author's full name (last name first), the full title of the book (underlined), the place of publication, the name of the publishing company, and the year of publication.
3. *For magazine articles:* Give the author's full name (last name first), the title of the article (in quotation marks), the full title of the magazine (underlined), the volume number (followed by a colon), the page number, and the publication date.

VI.

Finally, draw two more boxes on your paper. Label one *Introduction* and the other *Conclusion.* In the *Introduction* box, jot down how you will let your readers know the topic of the whole report. Also note reasons why your topic is interesting and worth reading about. In the *Conclusion* box, make notes that summarize the main points of your report. You may also jot down your final feelings about the topic. Or you may plan ways of considering the future in relation to the topic.

Reread the first and last paragraphs of "The Pants Invention" (page 127 and page 128) before you begin.

Writing a Report

On a separate sheet of paper, write a report on the topic you chose in "Getting Ready to Write" Part I. You may wish to review "The Pants Invention," on pages 127 through 128, before you begin. Use your answers to "Getting Ready to Write" (pages 131–132) to help you.

Once you have completed your report, be sure to add a *bibliography,* or a list of all the sources from which you got your information. The items in the bibliography should be in alphabetical order. You may wish to study the bibliography on page 129 before you begin. Use your answers to "Getting Ready to Write" Part V to help you.

SKILL BUILDING

Commas to Bring Ideas Together

Knowing how to use the comma enables you to combine many ideas into one smooth sentence. For example, notice the three short sentences that follow. Then notice how commas and a conjunction are used to combine them into a single sentence.

She gave me a funny look. She turned around. She walked out the door.

She gave me a funny look, turned around, and walked out the door.

Add commas to each group of short sentences to form *one* longer sentence. You also may add or cross out words, or you may change the word order where you feel it is necessary.

EXAMPLE: Dawn picked a topic. She gathered information. She wrote a report.

Dawn picked a topic, ~~She~~ gathered information, *and* ~~She~~ wrote a report.

1. He reached for the ball. He slipped on the grass. He fell on his face.

2. I asked her to help me. She just started laughing and walked out of the room.

3. Attila was the king of the Huns. He was a dwarf.

4. Thomas Edison invented the phonograph. He invented the light bulb. He invented the motion picture.

5. Linda Ronstadt was born in Tucson, Arizona. She studied at the University of Arizona.

6. In ancient Persia, people sometimes ate such things as zebra steaks. They ate gazelle livers. They ate smoked camel humps.

7. More men than women are rated as geniuses. Women have a higher average I.Q. than men.

8. In 1881 a man named David Lang walked into a field. He waved to his family. He vanished into thin air.

9. Napoleon was a fearless soldier. He was terrified of cats.

10. He wore an old suit. It was brown. It was double-breasted.

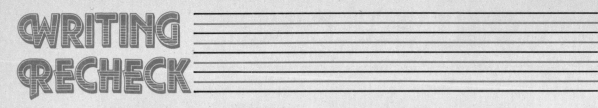

WRITING RECHECK

THINKING ABOUT WRITING

1. Reread your report. What kind of feeling does it convey? Does it show that you were interested in your subject? If not, add words and phrases that lend some enthusiasm to your writing.

2. Study the paragraphs in the body of your report—the paragraphs based on the questions you wrote. Do any of them contain too much or unnecessary information? If so, cross out sentences that you now see need to be removed. Do any of your paragraphs contain fewer than three sentences? If so, you probably need to add information.

3. Is your bibliography arranged in alphabetical order? Does it list all your sources of information? Did you place a comma after each piece of information within each item? If not, go back and make the necessary adjustments.

SKILL BUILDING

4. Take a careful look at your report. Are there any groups of short sentences that can be brought together into one long sentence by using commas? If so, rewrite these sentences on the lines below.

_____

_____

_____

_____

_____

_____

_____

_____

_____

5. Review your use of commas in your report. Correct any errors you find.

6. Rewrite your report on a separate sheet of paper. Make all the necessary corrections as you go along. You should have a neat, clean copy when you are through.

17

CWRITING KEYS

In the previous 16 lessons, you have done many different kinds of writing. You have written paragraphs, stories, poems, personal narratives—and several other forms besides.

One thing you may have learned from all the writing you have done is that an idea for writing can come from anywhere. It can even come from a simple picture—like that of the keys below. Not just one, but many types of writing can be triggered by this picture.

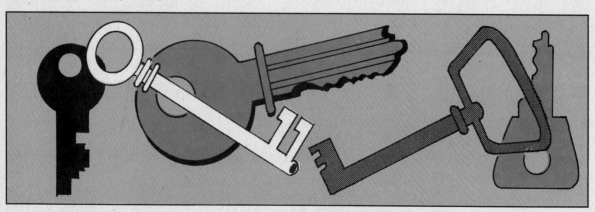

Read the selections that follow. Notice how many different forms of writing— all based on the same picture—are represented.

Thank You

An old man
walks
haltingly to his
front door.
He takes out his keys.
His hand
shakes and he drops them.
His son comes up from
behind, picks up
the keys, and opens the door.
The old man
enters,
too proud to say thank you.

The Lock

The first key-operated lock was invented about 4,000 years ago in ancient Egypt. It consisted of a large wooden bolt that was fastened to the outside of a gate. The first lock to be mass-produced was invented in 1865 by an American locksmith named Linus Yale, Jr. It was based on a principle similar to that of the ancient Egyptian lock.

The Zookeeper

They had made him the zookeeper. Sometimes he wished they hadn't. At times he wished they had gotten rid of all the creatures and closed the zoo.

Ten years before, they had gone off on a space probe and conquered a planet. Most of the natives had been killed. A handful had survived. They were brought back and put in the zoo.

Making his rounds, the zookeeper looked in the cages. The hideous creatures stared out at him. Their many-fingered hands clutched the bars, and their eyes were filled with hate. Some screamed and jabbered at him in their strange tongue.

He paused in front of one of the larger cages. One of the creatures was pulling itself up the bars. A group of children watched, fascinated.

At the sight of the zookeeper, the creature suddenly bellowed. The children's bright orange eyes flashed with fear. They backed away on tiny suction-cup feet.

With a bright green claw, the zookeeper took his keys from his belt. He rattled them at the Earth creature, making it howl with anger. The children laughed and danced with joy.

Twirling his keys on his claw, the zookeeper continued on his rounds. He smiled and began to hum an old Venusian tune.

THINKING ABOUT WHAT YOU HAVE READ

Answer in complete sentences.

1. Which selection is a fictional story? Which is an informative paragraph? What is the difference between the two forms? Explain your answer.

_____

_____

_____

2. At the beginning of "The Zookeeper," it seems as though a person from Earth has aliens from another planet in cages. But this is not the case. Who is the zookeeper, and where is he from? Who are the "creatures" in the cages?

_____

_____

3. What is described in the poem? Why do you think the old man may have been "too proud to say thank you"? Discuss your answers.

_____

_____

THINKING ABOUT WRITING

Editing a Composition

In past lessons you have studied many different kinds of writing problems. Some common problems are poor word choice, confusing word order in sentences, and repeated words and phrases. Now let's see if you can put all your writing skills to work for you.

Read the following selection carefully. Look for words, phrases, and sentences that you feel can be improved. Correct any errors and make any changes that seem necessary. If you need to rewrite an entire sentence, do so between the lines. A change has been made in the first sentence as an example.

The Lost Colony

In 1587 Governor John White settled ~~and landed~~ on Roanoke Island with 121 other colonists.

Among the colonists were White's wife, Mrs. White, his daughter, and his granddaughter (Virginia, the first child born to settlers in the New World).

Because more food and other things you might need and cloth were needed to survive the coming winter, White returned to England.

When White returned from England three years later with supplies, the colony he found had been deserted. The entire group of people who were living there had vanished and disappeared. The houses were all okay and all stood intact. There were no bodies that were dead. There were also of any sort of battle no signs. To this day, no one knows exactly for sure what happened or occurred to the colonists.

Getting Ready to Write

On pages 135 through 136, you saw how several different types of writing can be triggered by one picture. Another simple picture follows—a picture of an envelope that holds a letter. This picture is going to be the trigger for *two* different kinds of writing. The next few activities will help you get ready to write.

On a separate sheet of paper, answer the following questions in complete sentences.

1. A personal narrative tells a true experience from one's own life. Have you ever sent or received a very important letter? For example, have you ever received a letter that made you very mad, very happy, or very sad? Briefly describe what happened.

2. Where would you look in order to find out who invented paper, the envelope, and the postage stamp? Name at least two possible sources of information.

3. How would you describe a postage stamp without using the word *stamp?* What are some of the features you would mention? List them on your paper.

4. Is there a friendly letter you have been meaning to write but haven't gotten around to just yet? To whom would you write the letter? What would the letter say?

5. Can you make up a rhyming poem, a short story, or a play based on the following scene involving letters? Briefly, what would happen in your poem, story, or play? Describe the main events on the lines below the picture.

_____

_____

_____

_____

_____

_____

_____

_____

Writing Based on a "Letter Key"

On a separate sheet of paper, try your hand at *two* different forms of writing based on the picture of the stamped envelope on page 138. Choose any two of the following forms: description (without naming the object described), rhyming poem, short story, personal narrative, play, informative paragraph, friendly letter, summary, interview, or report. Use your answers to "Getting Ready to Write" to help you. You may also wish to study the models on pages 135–136 before you begin.

SKILL BUILDING

Review and Application

In earlier lessons you worked on improving your writing skills. These skills include capitalization, comma usage, end-of-sentence punctuation, correcting run-ons and fragments, and using pronouns properly.

I.

Read the following selection. Correct as many errors as you can find. There are more than 20 errors in all. The first error has been corrected for you.

The Night Caller

Do you believe in ghosts? If not, then how would you explain the following true story.

It was a cold winter night in ontario, Canada, during World war II and a middle-aged widow awoke from a troubled sleep to see she younger brother standing at the foot of her bed.

The woman was very frightened but her brother couldn't possibly be in her room she knew him was in england in the royal canadian Air Force.

The woman screamed her brother vanished

The woman's three children rushed into the room so sobbing she told them that her brother had been killed.

several days later, word came that the brother's Spitfire had been shot down over the english Channel. Had died on the same day—possibly at the same hour—that the woman had seen he "ghost" in her room

Was this "ghost" just the tail end of a nightmare. should we look for a more frightening explanation. Perhaps the brother, at the moment of his death, a message—a last cry for help—to him sister in canada. maybe such a thing is impossible, but how can we know for sure!

II.

Add commas where they are needed in the following sentences.

1. Walt Disney the cartoonist was once an ambulance driver.

2. Whitcomb Judson for example invented the zipper in 1893.

3. The hummingbird is the only bird that can fly backwards and it is the only one that can hover in the same spot.

4. "Sue did you know that Pancho Villa the famous Mexican revolutionary once invaded the United States?"

5. If left to nature the tea plant would grow into a tree 30 feet (9.1 meters) high.

6. Napoleon Bonaparte was a short pudgy man.

7. "I have heard Mandy that Kris Kristofferson the singer and actor was once an outstanding football player."

8. One day in 1940 a man waded into the Mississippi River swam south for 292 miles (470 kilometers) finally became exhausted and crawled onto shore.

THINKING ABOUT WRITING

1. Reread the two pieces of writing you did for this lesson. Which, in your opinion, is more effective? Here's a slightly different question: Which one do you like better? Explain your answers on the lines below.

    _____

    _____

    _____

2. Now exchange your writing with a classmate. Have your classmate choose the piece he or she thinks is more effective. Also ask which piece he or she likes better. Do your choices match your classmate's? Discuss the reasons for the choices each of you made.

3. Compare the writing you did for this lesson with the writing you completed for Lessons 1 through 5 in this book. On the lines below, list three ways in which you feel your writing has improved. Then list three areas that still need improvement.

    _____

    _____

    _____

SKILL BUILDING

4. Put a check (√) next to any of the following errors you find in your two pieces of writing. Then make the necessary corrections on your paper. The page numbers in parentheses ( ) tell you where to turn in this book for review.

    _____ capitalization and end punctuation (pp. 16 and 24)

    _____ redundancy (p. 36)   _____ commas (pp. 64–133)

    _____ run-on sentences (p. 31)   _____ pronoun usage (pp. 46–47, 55–57)

    _____ word order (p. 4)   _____ verb tense (pp. 38–40)